POLISHED STEEL:
LESSONS FROM THE DOJO

by Shaz Davis

COPYRIGHT

ACKNOWLEDGEMENTS

THIS BOOK WOULD not have been possible if it were not for Sensei and the numerous students who walked the path with Sensei either fleetingly or over several years - or even decades - each providing the stimulus and environment for these teachings.

My thanks goes to all of you who touched our dojo-related lives bringing joy, humour - and lessons.

Russel Brownlee, my writing coach, had the unenviable job of helping me find my writing mojo and encouraged me to make the time to write when that seemed impossible.

Also my sincere thanks to everyone who has been subjected to various iterations of these stories for comments, feedback and proof reading. And to my many writer friends who each provide inspiration to write and be creative though the work and posts they share.

FOREWORD

TRAINING IN a traditional dojo is only 50 percent technique. Students sign up to learn self-defence or a particular art, but stay because of the holistic body, mind, and spirit lessons that blend with the teachings in almost every class.

This is a work of historical non-fiction. All the stories actually occurred and are recounted to the best of my recollection, or as retold to me by Sensei or the students involved. Some of the settings might be embellished a little, and the names of those involved could be either accurate or changed.

Sensei has personally taught and enhanced the lives of more than 5,000 students, so any first name could cover a number of possible students and should not be considered an identifier, as it could be another student or an arbitrary name.

My warm thanks to Sensei, aka Lao Tse or Bob Davies, for all the lessons spanning nearly two decades, and to everyone who travelled the path, however fleeting or long, and trained a while with Sensei. It was a pleasure to have your company on Sensei's lifelong journey of learning and self-improvement - living the motto of developing spirituality through physicality.

For those who haven't met Sensei, I hope these stories bring a knowing smile and resonate with your own experiences with your Sensei, or add to your experiences based on any training floor.

Gateless dojo gate
An invitation to enter
Path of life-long learning

TABLE OF CONTENTS

LEAVE YOUR EGO
WITH YOUR SHOES

THE WEATHERED SIGN AT the dojo door read: Leave your ego with your shoes at the door. Looking dapper and exactly like the accomplished big-name lawyer he was, Suren glanced at the sign as he strode past, hand extended with a confident smile to greet Sensei, and didn't give the sign another thought.

Sensei always interviewed prospective students and would chat amiably in the shade of the dojo veranda discussing their training interests and motivations. This helped Sensei assess the person's suitability as a potential student, and provided an opportunity to suggest the appropriate training options for what they hoped to achieve.

Most interviews lasted more than an hour and the meeting with Suren was no exception, even though Suren was surreptitiously looking at his watch and mentally rescheduling his afternoon as time wore on. As discussions were drawing to a close, Sensei invited Suren to have a look at the dojo; an opportunity Suren graciously accepted.

For those new to dojo etiquette, entering Sensei's dojo correctly was a lot like waltzing through a field peppered, somewhat overzealously, with land mines. There was only a slight chance of coming out the other side unscathed.

Sensei always tried to guide people through the process, explaining why each step was important. Most people assumed it was a simple enough process (or that rules would not apply to them as visitors) and put a foot wrong before Sensei had a chance to guide them through the process.

There was a raised wooden walkway (which you are supposed to stand on in bare feet, not in your shoes) and a bench for your shoes, with a helpful sign that read: For the covers of your feet, not the cover of your seat.

Suren had read the first sign about leaving his shoes at the door, and eager to impress Sensei, he stepped up on the wooden walkway and turned around to sit on the "bench" to take off his shoes.

Before Suren had a chance to sit on the flimsy shoe bench,

Sensei bellowed a sharp "NO!" that would have stopped a rampaging lion in mid-attack.

Sensei explained the process to Suren and passed him a cloth to wipe the shoe prints off the wooden boards.

A little more nervously, Suren tried again. He stood next to the raised platform, stepped out of his shoes onto the floor, put his shoes on the shoe bench and stepped up onto the wooden platform, only to be greeted by an exasperated Sensei.

Sensei explained that Suren had stood in his bare feet on the dirty floor, and then stepped up onto the boards, bringing the dirt from the floor onto the boards. Sensei sent a red-faced Suren off to wipe the boards and wash his feet before trying to enter the dojo again.

Suren wiped the boards for the second time, and walked to the end of the veranda to the tap to wash his feet, and walked back, still barefoot, along the veranda to find a displeased Sensei looking at him.

It was fourth time lucky for Suren. He took his shoes with him to the tap, washed his feet, and dried them with his designer socks, before putting his shoes back on without socks. He walked to the boards and stepped up onto the boards as he took each foot out of its shoe, and placed the shoes on the shoe bench.

Then all he had to do was bow at the entrance under Sensei's guidance and step, with the correct foot leading, into the dojo. Sensei showed Suren where the shomen, or front of the dojo, was and explained that a person would never step into or out of the dojo with their back turned to the shomen. For this dojo that meant stepping with the right leg first when entering.

After a quick look around the dojo, Sensei showed Suren how to turn and bow at the door and step out with the left leg leading to keep his heart facing the shomen.

After that introduction to training and dojo life, Sensei did not expect to see Suren again. But Suren was intrigued that a Sensei could be more intimidating than a court judge or a high-powered lawyer, and he figured he might just learn a thing or two if he managed to leave his ego at the door - which he did for several years until his law practice became too busy.

Neat row of shoes wait
Patiently without ego
Dawn floods the sky

COUNT TO TEN

OUR INTERMEDIATE SWORD CLASS often started with a fairly large focus on basic techniques. A regular was maki uchi, a rotating strike or forward cut that accommodates the helmet worn by the samurai in battle.

Sensei would have us line up in order of seniority at the start of the class and start off with maki uchi. He would count to ten while we executed the technique to the count. Then the most senior student would count to ten, then the next most senior student, and so on, until everyone had counted to ten. The counting was, of course, in Japanese.

If anyone made a mistake with the count, Sensei would take back the lead and start counting again: ichi, ni, san, chi, go, roku, sichi, hachi, kyu, JU. The last number was always louder, to signify the end of the ten-count and remind the next person in line to take over, and another round of counting and techniques would follow.

Once the newer students moved into the intermediate

class, it didn't take them long to realise they needed to learn to count to ten in Japanese. Most learnt to count along in their head with everyone else and got it right within a few turns.

But one older gentlemanly student, Monty, just couldn't get the counting to stick in his head under pressure. In the beginner's class, they were allowed to count in English or weren't asked to count at all. When it was Monty's turn to count he would lose the count halfway, if not before.

Sensei kept a poker face and upped the pressure; starting and re-starting the count until everyone, but Monty, was counting comfortably.

After a few classes of this, Monty tried writing the counting sequence on the back of his hand so that he wouldn't be the cause of the class doing endless repetitions of maki uchi. But Monty soon discovered that he couldn't read anything written on his hands because the backs of his hands were sideways, not facing upwards when holding the sword.

A little disillusioned, but not dissuaded, Monty returned to class with plan b. The counting sequence was now written on paper securely taped to his bokuto (a wooden training sword). But plan b wasn't perfect either.

"Ichi, ni, san...," said Monty, followed by a long uncomfortable pause...

"Chi..."

Another pause with Monty doing a strange technique and starting the move before he had begun to count; something students are taught not to do because the count represents your signal to move -- the opening to strike.

Monty's writing was too small and he couldn't read his special crib notes at the distance he was supposed to hold the sword from his body, so he was aberrating the technique and counting painfully slowly. Fortunately for Monty (and us),

Sensei was in front of the class facing the shomen (front of the dojo), like the rest of us, and didn't see what Monty was doing.

The next class involved plan c. Monty arrived with much larger crib note taped to his bokuto. Plan c worked reasonably well for maki uchi. There were discernible pauses in Monty's counting, but the numbers flowed well enough that we soon moved onto other techniques.

But Monty's luck ran out. The class included doing paired kata and Monty was soon paired off with Sensei, who couldn't help but notice the large note on Monty's bokuto.

Suffice it to say that Sensei did not count to ten before exploding, and the class went back to maki uchi with no crib notes.

Joyous class clown smiles
Pleased despite his haplessness
Others fret and frown

POLISHED STEEL

IT'S EARLY ON A dark, wintry Saturday morning. The sort of hour any sane person would be curled up comfortably in bed. It's cold, and yes, we'd all rather be sleeping under a cosy blanket, or doing just about anything – absolutely anything but stamping shoeless feet on the well-worn Oregon pine floor, trying to keep warm.

It's our combined sword class, a time when the different student levels train together, a class where the senior students get to focus on the basics and help the others along. It's usually a class the seniors dread, as it takes them to new levels of tedium and frustration. It tests whether they have what it takes to really be a senior: Patience, perseverance, and a willingness to help others along the path.

The seniors are stoic. The lower levels are excited. For them, a combined class means new work, new learning; exposure to the seniors and the exciting stuff - the skills they want to learn.

The class starts with a short warm-up and then moves onto the suburi where we revise (or learn) the basic techniques in our sword art. The crisp command cuts through the air: "Jodan no kamae."

We're facing each other in two lines, swords engaged. We all step back smartly into the upper level on guard position with the sword handle positioned on the hairline and running back across the head – taking care to ensure the blade remain straight ready to cut the attacker in front of us.

"Seigan no kamae," rings out and we all step forward in unison, back to the on-guard posture – sword held out in front, with the tip height positioned at just the right height to ensure that the opponent can't accurately read the length of the sword. Sword tips crossed precisely at the right place.

Sensei is a pedantic and demanding teacher. He corrects by providing a general reminder or example. It's always general, almost never person-specific, and the students are never sure whether a correction is aimed at them in particular or not. Usually, this ensures that everyone listens carefully.

This morning, the class is reminded that the back foot must not move, or even twitch, until the front foot has stepped past and landed on the floor. The seniors sigh inwardly as they listen, for the umpteenth time, to Sensei's explanation of how it would compromise stability on the battlefield (as opposed to a nice, forgiving, smooth, wooden training floor) and we eventually get back to training.

Jodan no kamae. Seigan no kamae, jodan no kamae. Seigan no kamae... On we go for several minutes. The seniors move confidently; totally comfortable with the move and convinced, with ingrained body knowledge, that they're doing it correctly.

As time passes with each increasingly painful repetition,

the anguish (for some physical, for most mental) is palpable. Most of us know that we're going to do jodan no kamae until the person doing it incorrectly finally gets it right. It usually only takes a couple of minutes for this to happen.

Jodan no kamae. Seigan no kamae... The seniors glance down the lines. More and more of the lower levels check their stances and adjust their movement to watch their foot to see if they are the guilty one. Eventually, even the seniors feel their confidence wane, and they too check their moves.

Finally secure that they are not the culprit they scan the ranks again to find out which idiot is too dense to at least bother to check their moves.

Sixty minutes later, the entire class is focused on a very elusive inner peace and willing that arty blonde, hair pulled in a wispy ponytail, to realise that perhaps, possibly, it just might be her. Venomous glances and murderous thoughts are sent alternatively at the blonde, and then at Sensei, but to no avail. Jodan no kamae. Seigan no kamae. Jodan no kamae...

Yup, that blonde's foot continued to move at the wrong time. Jodan no kamae. Seigan no kamae...

With relief, we finally hear: Yame, the instruction to stop; then: Noto, to bow and re-sheath our swords. The end of our 90-minute class has arrived. An entire class of jodan no kamae – and a whole lot of students (bar one) who will never, ever, move their foot incorrectly ever again.

A few will have also learned that they could keep going when they felt like giving up, and a handful will have tried to execute their very best technique on each command. Sometimes, you need to apply grit and hard work to achieve a beautiful polished steel blade - or a polished technique.

Cicada's chorus
Loudly in the summer heat
The samurai waits

IF YOU DON'T KNOW: ASK

SENSEI HAD A PRESENCE about him that seemed magnified and multiplied on the dojo floor. He cut a daunting figure, and during gradings and evaluations he seemed to glower at you from the desk and bristle with annoyance that grew with every error.

Evaluations were nerve-wracking times - deliberately planned as such to prepare Sensei's students for any difficult situation they might encounter off the dojo floor.

One particular brown belt evaluation had been progressing reasonably well until Sensei threw a curveball and asked for a technique that was on the grading requirements, but had not been taught in class.

At this level the syllabus is huge and the number of techniques the students are expected to know is dauntingly long - so the students were not entirely sure whether they had been taught the move or not - and assumed that if Sensei was asking for the move, it would be one they had been taught.

Sensei knew otherwise, but wasn't about to let on.

Sensei called out the instruction. The students stood still, staring straight ahead. They had trained with Sensei long enough to know better than to try and glance to the side to pick up tips from what others might be doing.

Sensei repeated the instruction with a discernible note of annoyance entering his strident voice. The students hesitated, minds whirling. They seemed to decide, in unison, that it would be wiser to do the wrong technique, any technique had to be better than standing still doing nothing at all.

Three different and incorrect versions emerged from the three students on the floor. Sensei snapped at them and repeated the instruction for the students to try again, and again. His voice got angrier at each incorrect attempt.

After ten anxious minutes, which felt more like an hour to the harried students, Sensei said the move in English rather than Japanese.

This prompted the students, a couple of whom were now literally quivering with fear and nervous energy, to attempt a few more moves with Sensei expressing disapproval at every turn. They even got the move right a couple of times, but not consistently, so Sensei pushed on.

Eventually, Warren summoned enough courage to stop trying.

Sensei stared hard and said: "Warren, you're not moving!"

"I... I... I don't know this move, Sensei." Warren stammered, sounding a lot braver than he felt.

"If you don't know something, why don't you just ask?" bellowed Sensei in response and proceeded to break down the move and teach the students how to do it.

It is a lesson Warren has never forgotten. If you don't know - just ask. It might be difficult to admit you don't know something and you might fear ridicule, but everything runs much smoother if you bite the bullet and ask.

Do not keep quiet when you don't know, or don't understand. If you don't know: ASK. That is how you learn and grow.

Sometimes in the quiet
The answers come unbidden
Certain from within

WHAT'S IN A SHOUT?

WHEN MARY FIRST STARTED training with Sensei, she signed up for classes in the gentle, slow flowing art of t'ai chi. It was tranquil, calm, and left her feeling blissful afterwards.

The longer she trained, the more time Mary spent around the dojo and the more exposure she had to the other arts that Sensei taught. Even though her form contained a few kicks and punches, the other arts were nothing like t'ai chi.

The strangest thing, for Mary, was all the shouting. The sword students used various shouts that seemed to alternate through Ay, Ya, and Toh. Toh was usually at the end of the kata sequence. The other art just seemed to use a longer Aaa, like the a in a b c.

The students used to get groused at if they forgot to shout, although some would just say Aaah in a bored monotone barely above a whisper and a few, feeling uncomfortable with the requirement, would mouth the sound, but not actually voice it at all.

Intrigued by the requirement for these arts Mary eventually plucked up the courage to ask Sensei what all the shouting was about.

"Shouting?" Sensei broke into a ready smile. "Oh, the kakegoe! Most dojo would call them kiai. It translates roughly as a spirit shout. It has two basic uses: Either to provide courage and motivation to the person shouting, much like a power lifter would grunt or shout as he lifted a heavy weight, or to intimidate the opponent.

Sensei went on to explain that in the sword art, the sounds are also linked to an esoteric form of Buddhism, and something to do with mantra, seed symbols, and disrupting an adversary's energy – all of which was lost on Mary at the time.

"A good kakegoe comes from the dan tien," said Sensei, reverting to the Chinese equivalent of the hara, so that Mary could put that into context, "and not from the throat."

Mary thanked Sensei for his time and explanation but was still sceptical about the whole shouting business. She couldn't see how shouting Aaa at anyone - even in her loudest AAAAaaaa - would intimidate anybody. She certainly found most of the other student's attempts ineffectual and decided it was just plain weird. But then a lot of things around the dojo were weird, but not necessarily wrong.

A few weeks later Sensei arranged for a beach training session for everyone, and Mary was walking with Sensei and a few other students. As the group started to climb a dune, the head of a fierce looking German Shepherd appeared over the top of the dune, barking, teeth bared.

Just as Mary was about to react in fright, Sensei let out a fearsome sound that reverberated in the air and seemed to go on forever. It froze everyone in their tracks, except for the

German Shepherd, who turned and ran off with his tail between his legs.

It seemed to Mary as though Sensei's kakegoe followed the dog, chasing him further away, like a long roll of thunder.

Although Mary didn't say anything, she was impressed. Sensei had illustrated the power of a good kakegoe, and now Mary understood that the shouting was like any other part of the arts Sensei taught. Not easy to learn, but effective when you eventually got it right.

It wasn't too long after the beach incident that Mary decided to try a few of the other arts Sensei taught. Her interest was piqued, and she wanted to learn more about them.

Shrill silence
Stopping the heart
A warrior's shout

HAPPY NEW YEAR

AS THE END OF Edmund's first year of training approached, he was looking forward to the final class of the year and taking some time out to be with family and friends. Young Edmund had not learned enough of Sensei's ways to be concerned when Sensei promised a wonderful celebratory combined class for the last class of the year.

Edmund arrived at the dojo, eager as ever. He changed into his gi, or training uniform, and stepped bravely and unwittingly onto the dojo floor. All the students were there, running through stretches, chatting amiably, and glowing with a combination of the festive spirit and summer heat.

"Sensei must be cleaning," thought Edmund when saw various wooden weapons -jo, bo, and escrima sticks- standing around the perimeter of the dojo.

The meaning of the small change in the dojo that Edmund noticed wasn't clear - so no alarm bells went off.

Sensei called the class to attention. Led the floor teeming

with students through a warm-up, and like so many classes, Sensei began this one began with a punching drill: choku tsuki - a straight, forward punch to the chest.

Ichi, ni, san, chi...

San ju ichi... Hachi ju san...

Kyu ju kyu... Hyaku!

"Phew, one hundred. That will get the blood flowing," thought Edmund as he watched Sensei stride over to the first weapon leaning against the wall and knock it to the floor - while still counting.

Curious, thought Edmund - but he was getting used to Sensei's strange behaviour.

Undaunted, or simply slow to understand, Edmund happily punched to Sensei's count until ni hyaku - two hundred. And Sensei walked over and knocked down the second wooden weapon.

At this point, Edmund, and probably a number of other newer students began to figure out what was going on. There was a lot of surreptitious eye-swiveling and head cocking as they tried to count the number of weapons line up around the dojo walls.

Sensei had, of course, arranged the weapons so that no matter where you stood at least half would not be visible, so it was guess work at best for everyone, except for those who had done a final year end class before.

The count that night continued relentlessly - reaching 500 and then 1000. The students sweated on, fighting boredom and fatigue, executing choku tsuki after chock tsuki to 1500, and on, until they reached a resounding 2000 and Sensei knocked over the last wooden weapon.

2000 chest punches - not at all coincidental that the year 2000 was the year being rung in.

Edmund had a new experience - not to mention sore arms - to share with his friends over the break, but also a sense of euphoria at having achieved a fairly daunting task.

Limiting beliefs
Create a limited life
Comfort zones are banned

RUNNING WAS
NOT THE LESSON

OUR REGULAR WEEK-LONG training camp, or gasshuku, was a much-anticipated event - feared and enjoyed in equally intense measure by those who took part. The venue was tucked away somewhere amongst remote and rugged mountains. The timing was either during the coldest part of winter or the height of summer -- and those who survived a gasshuku returned with much-exaggerated tales of endurance, fortitude, and ardour. These stories were eagerly shared between junior and senior students alike, and gasshuku was often the training highlight of the year.

Edmund's first gasshuku was in winter at Wagendrift Dam. It began at "zero-dark-horrible o'clock" with a wake-up call for all the students.

Staggering outside with bleary eyes, Edmund discovered that winter on gasshuku involved sparkly white frost twinkling in his torchlight. For somebody raised in a coastal town, it was a sure sign of the biblical apocalypse, or a cold, uncaring universe, depending on your personal views.

Gasshuku mornings started early, every morning, and they all started with what Sensei called a Wu-Shin shuffle. The shuffle was, in fact, a run. This first morning the run proceeded directly up from the bungalows at the water's edge up to the tar-sealed main access road to the dam, and back again.

But the devil was in the unspoken detail. The concrete strip road up from the dam to the road was nicknamed Heartbreak Hill. As the name implies, it was a relentless and long uphill slog.

Not being a mountain goat, Edmund proceeded as fast as possible, which wasn't awfully fast but around average. Up the hill and down again where he enjoyed a heart-stoppingly refreshing dip in the inky black pre-sunrise dam water. "F-f-f-f-r-r-eezing!" was frequently muttered.

The run was a precursor to a full day's worth of solid, hard training in the sun, and the run bleached the willpower right out of Edmund, requiring a lot of determination to keep going.

So Edmund did what any self-respecting intelligent student would do and secretly started a running programme before the next gasshuku. Edmund bought a good pair of running shoes and ran, and ran, and ran some more until he was ready in time for gasshuku number two.

When the students set off on the first day's run, Edmund wore a satisfied smile, along with his beanie, gloves, and more. Eager to enjoy the fruits of his clever plan, Edmund flew up and down Heartbreak Hill. So much so that Sensei was still running to the top when Edmund was on the way down.

Edmund was pleased to see Sensei approach him while he was waiting for the rest of the gang at the bottom of the hill. Sensei was beaming at Edmund, which should have set off some warning bells.

Sensei congratulated Edmund on his run and asked Edmund to follow him to the main bungalow. A tiny alarm did start to sound in Edmund's brain then. Sensei rummaged in a box and gave Edmund two blue ankle weights, saying: "Tomorrow's run - enjoy these."

Having never seen ankle weights before, Edmund soon became intimately acquainted with the velcro attachments from hell.

Running, or even running well, was not the point; finding the mental and physical strength to enthusiastically face a day of hard training after a breakfast buffet of heartbreak and exhaustion was. Lesson learned (for Edmund anyway).

Physical challenge
Up Heartbreak Hill you shall run
Frosty winter's morn'

BOREDOM AND PAIN

THE SUN WAS BAKING down, and Sensei decided that outdoor training would allow everyone to enjoy the summer afternoon and get the benefit of some fresh air and sunshine.

Josh and Ben were doing paired sword kata, taking turns to squint into the sun as they swapped roles, when Sensei called a stop to their training and launched into a gasshuku story.

The hapless participants of this particular gasshuku had the typical training camp joy of a 5km run every morning. But Sensei, as usual, added a touch of difficulty. The senior students, much like the warrior monks from Mount Hiei, had the pleasure of doing their morning run while carrying their weapons in front of them.

Ben had only been training with Sensei for a year, and he was enjoying the story and the break in training. Josh, on the other hand, had been training with Sensei for quite a bit longer, and he knew that a story like this was usually a precursor to trying out this rediscovered form of torture.

Sensei went into detail. Of course the student's weren't just holding the weapons comfortably. They were holding their arm straight out at shoulder height and had a firm grip on the very end of the bo, or long staff, with the other end extended out in front at shoulder height.

Josh grimaced, and right on cue, Sensei said,"It's not an easy thing to do - let's try it." Ben and Josh went to get their bo, only to be stopped in their tracks and sent to fetch their o' naginata - a longer and heavier weapon.

After several minutes of holding the weapon out in front Sensei then asked the class to turn the weapon in small tight circles in front of them, rather than hold the weapon still.

Just when you thought it couldn't get any harder, Sensei had the knack of making a slight change to take you to new heights of mental anguish and determination. Ben's face was bright red, and he was struggling to stay focused. Josh was stoic and doing his utmost to empty his mind of the pain, the tedium, and the excruciating muscle burn...

"What are the two things that destroy love? I've mentioned this before?" asked Sensei.

Sensei's earlier talk had made an impression on Josh, but this was a welcome respite and he wasn't going to volunteer the information too readily. Sensei had said that the boredom that comes with predictability in a partner could lend itself to making someone else seem more exciting and therefore more attractive. Sensei had also said that physical pain could kill love. A person in pain is grumpy and hurting, and neither are pleasant to be around nor is that person able to relax and share time and appreciation in a normal way.

Sensei honed in on Ben. "What are the two things?"

"Sorry, Sensei, I don't remember," admitted Ben.

Sensei's gaze moved to Josh.

"Boredom and pain," volunteered Josh.

"That's right! That's what you learn to fight with this exercise too - boredom and pain," said Sensei as he indicated that it was time to raise the o' naginata in the air again, and started the count from ichi in slow, painful, tight circles.

It wasn't long before the burn of the forearm muscles set in again, and shoulders and arms added their alto scream to the painful chorus. Everybody was sweating and wavering - and finding new ways to overcome boredom and pain.

Summer love lingers
Long shadows of sunset fade
And die quietly

THE BEST WAY TO WIN A FIGHT

SENSEI ALWAYS USED TO say that the best way to win a fight was to avoid the confrontation in the first place. That was his reasoned excuse for all the run training on gasshuku - to make sure his students could run away from danger, if necessary.

Simon had often heard Sensei say: "If you're ever faced with an aggressor, your first and best defence is to run as fast as you can."

This was also drilled into students as the dojo ABC's - an acronym for avoid, block, and counter. Sensei had various drills he used to train his students to avoid the attack, block the attack, and then counter the attack. For Simon, it was one thing learning this in theory, but the lesson really hit home harder when Sensei provided a real life example.

One particular Tuesday evening after work, Sensei was

teaching a class in his dojo in the poorer end of town where the rent was, of necessity, cheaper. The dojo was on the first floor in a semi-industrial area that had some rough and tough people passing by on the streets below.

Simon was amongst the students, lined up facing a row of windows looking out over a seedy alley, flanked by grimy brick buildings. Sensei had his back to the windows, facing the class. He was busy explaining the detail of a kata, when a brick, thrown from below, crashed through the windowpane, spraying glass onto a section of the dojo floor.

Simon was about the rush to the window to see who had the audacity to interrupt class. Several others students thought it a good idea to head for the stairs to find, and confront, the perpetrators, but Sensei remained focused on his class.

He did not flinch or even turn his head. He just instructed the class to continue and carried on with the lesson while calmly asking two senior students, who were warming up on the side of the dojo floor, to clean up the glass.

The person, or people, below had hoped to disrupt the class and get a reaction from Sensei and his students, but they got neither. In one simple action of not rising to the bait, Sensei illustrated perfectly how to avoid confrontation and win without fighting.

Indignation sparks
Then cools to calm awareness
It takes two to fight

THAT'S NOT SHODAN

MARY'S EXPLORATION INTO SWORD training was never easy. She had a natural ability when it came to t'ai chi, but sword training was a different scenario. It required a lot of hard work and perseverance - and, perhaps, that is part of what attracted her to the art. It was something she really needed to work at to master, which brought a tangible sense of accomplishment - and there was the attraction of that elusive ability to read people and respond before they attacked.

The dojo's early training in Katori Shinto Ryu was under Hatakeyama Sensei, through affiliations with a Dutch dojo. Our small group would either go to Holland to train or host the Dutch Sensei at our dojo for training.

The previous year, the first three of Sensei's students were awarded shodan - their first level black belt. All of these students had trained for a number of years under Sensei in another art, with a range of weapons, and were much faster learners than a slow t'ai chi student like Mary.

But by the following year, Mary had put in a lot of training and she felt she was ready to try for shodan and so did Sensei. It was around the time that the movie, The Last Samurai, was released and the dojo membership had swelled to unprecedented numbers (for sword-related classes anyway).

When the time came for Mary's evaluation, she was paired off with one of the shodan students to go through the kata - in front of everyone. Most of the kata went well enough. Not flawlessly, but passable.

For the last set of kata, the Dutch Sensei decided to pair Mary off with a different shodan student. Unbeknown to the Dutch Sensei, this particular student had missed almost all of the last six months worth of classes - and was more than a little rusty on kata sequences, especially the more advanced kata.

They got through the first few kata without too much trouble, but on the last few, his hesitancy and uncertainty were palpable. That meant Mary didn't know how to respond and floundered. As she bowed out of the last kata the Dutch Sensei roared out: "That's not shodan" in front of everyone.

Mary understood immediately and died inside with acute embarrassment. Fortunately, the Dutch Sensei's English wasn't always clear and most people, including Mary's Sensei, had no idea what he said.

It was an interesting lesson. Up until that point, Mary had always held the naive belief that the belt or rank you held in any martial art was a fair evaluation of your ability. It mostly held true in Sensei's dojo, but this taught Mary that life in any dojo is as likely to be as unfair as life outside the dojo. You need ability, hard work, and a fair shot in order to succeed - and sometimes circumstances don't offer you that fair shot.

This was an interesting precursor to requesting a nidan evaluation in Katori Shinto Ryu under Sugino Sensei via a dojo in Switzerland a few years later. Sensei had decided to move from training under Hatakeyama Sensei to training under Sugino Sensei, and as his students, we obviously followed suit.

A handful of Sensei's students had been awarded shodan the previous year under Sugino Sensei, but despite knowing the required kata and moving acceptably for the level, they were denied the opportunity to grade for nidan as the system dictated that there had to be a two-year training period between the two - irrespective of actual knowledge and ability.

And that's where Mary lost all interest is chasing any more grades, levels, belts, or external recognition. Training (and life) is about developing abilities and growing as a person, not the concessions or recognition other people may, or may not, decide to bestow on you at any particular point in time.

Pink cherry blossoms
Bloom in brief beauty and fall
Cut of folded steel

TRUST YOUR ABILITY

GRADINGS, OR EVALUATIONS, ARE designed to test the participants both mentally and physically. Apart from testing a student's knowledge and his or her ability to execute techniques, evaluations, especially those under the close scrutiny of Sensei, test how well a student performs under pressure.

Sensei was a master of many things and controlling the dojo environment and creating pressure were two of his finely honed skills; as a result, evaluations were viewed with trepidation. The less students had trained and prepared, the less the participant's fluttering squad of butterflies were able to fly in formation.

In order to pass, students had to get 75 percent or more in some systems or make fewer than five material errors in others. Sensei often told the class that it was crazy that a doctor could pass with 50 percent and be let loose to practice medicine not knowing half the medical syllabus - and he wasn't about to allow the rush to mediocrity in his dojo.

During one particular evaluation, Sensei sat at the middle of the table near the shomen, leading the evaluation panel with several senior students. Five would-be brown belts were up for their test with the usual mix of prepared and unprepared, and pressure performers and those who performed well in class, but faltered miserably under pressure.

Thomas stood out amongst them. He had clearly trained hard for this evaluation and was performing comfortably and confidently. Any mistakes he made were small and insignificant for his level and everyone watching thought he would comfortably get his brown belt on his first attempt.

The change in expectations between a green belt with three stripes and a brown belt was large -- so large that almost nobody got through without a re-evaluation. But Thomas knew his stuff and cruised through the first hour of basic techniques and paired drills.

Thomas was called up to do his kata. He stepped up, bowed, and called out a crisp Saifa and started. A few moves into the kata there was some audible stage whispering from Sensei to the rest of the panel. Then a heavy sigh from Sensei, as he slapped his pen down on the table and made a show of tearing up a sheet of paper into teeny tiny pieces - with the efficiency and noise of a shredding machine on steroids.

Thomas had turned to the side for part of the kata just before the whispering started and his performance had faltered slightly. By the time the paper was torn up, he was back to facing the evaluation panel and visibly lost confidence as he watched his angry-looking Sensei shred what he assumed was his evaluation sheet.

The formerly confident Thomas moved hesitantly and

made uncharacteristic mistakes as he started to over think moves and tried to figure out what he might have done to make Sensei furious enough to tear up his evaluation paper.

Evaluations usually last three or more hours (or ran over several days for the higher grades), and Thomas' performance fell apart in the last hour as he stopped trusting his performance, as well as his preparation and knowledge.

A few weeks later Sensei presented the results and gave Thomas a sheet with his re-evaluation requirements. Thomas gaped and said, "But Sensei, I thought you tore up my evaluation sheet!"

"Why would I do that when you were doing so well, Thomas? If you know your work well, why would you let the presumed opinion of someone else throw you off balance?" said Sensei.

Incense curls slowly
Bearing prayers to the sky
Summer sun smiles down

TACKLE THE HARD STUFF FIRST

ONE OF THE DEFINING characteristics of training with Sensei was that he always kept you guessing. You never knew exactly where you stood or what to expect. And if you arrived at the point where you thought you had the system sussed out, you found that the rules had been changed without notice.

At around brown belt level, Sensei would ask each student to choose a weapon they wanted to focus on for training. It wasn't that they wouldn't cover the other weapons, but they could choose which one they wanted to focus on first.

Simon was looking forward to this. He'd watched the senior students training with the bo - a long wooden staff - and felt that was what he wanted to learn. It looked stately and controlled, not to mention, practical.

Besides he'd had a go with the nunchaku and hitting

himself on the head or body wasn't quite what he had in mind as an intimidating form of self-defence. There was as much chance of inflicting damage to himself as an assailant if he was flinging the nunchaku around.

Simon was clear what his choice of weapon would be - and it wasn't the nunchaku. When the day finally came, and Sensei asked Simon to choose, Simon said unhesitatingly, "I choose the bo."

Most students hem and haw when asked and Simon's certainly was not lost on Sensei. He replied saying: "Okay, take the nunchaku, then."

Simon was annoyed with Sensei at first and put out that he wasn't allowed to start with his first choice of weapon. But there was a well-intended lesson behind that instruction.

On the floor in the dojo, and off the floor in real life, sometimes you need to tackle the hard things. Simon slowly discovered that there was an advantage to doing the things he disliked first. Once he tackled the hard stuff, the rest was both easy and enjoyable.

The weight of adversity
Oppressive. Impossible.
A new day dawns

THERE ARE NO RULES IN A KNIFE FIGHT

SENSEI WOULD OFTEN ENCOURAGE his students to explore other combat forms to improve their skills and their understanding of the dynamics of weapons; also to expose them to other instructors, different styles, and a wide range of combatants.

One such event was a knife-fighting seminar, run by Tom Sotis from the US. Tom Sotis has an impressive CV that includes training the US Marines in deadly hand-to-hand combat, where all that matters is staying alive. His style, called 'Amok!', is brutal and effective. It also results in a lot of bruises from training with short wooden knives.

Sensei exhorted and encouraged his students to attend - and many did, Mary included, but not without some apprehension.

The seminar involved learning a range of close quarter

combat drills with the knife, which was practised in pairs, occasionally swapping partners until the participants had each drill more or less mastered.

At one point, we were each given a chance to spar with another participant. In theory, the first person to draw blood and inflict and injury (imagined in this case as we were using wooden training knives) was the winner.

All this was happening during a period in Mary's training where she was learning about sen - or seizing the initiative - and that's what Mary did when it was her turn to spar.

As the pair walked out onto the training floor, which was, in fact, a school hall, Mary focused her intention on attacking first as the only means to survive.

She bowed, and immediately seized the initiative and attacked, charging in to cover the distance and score a clean imaginary cut right out of the starting blocks. A good nick on the forearm, right by a vein or artery - something that would weep copious amounts of blood at any rate, if the weapons were real.

Objective achieved... or so Mary thought.

But it happened so quickly that her slick and fast victory was a win of no win because Mary's opponent simply ignored the mock slash and continued to circle her ready to attack, causing Mary's satisfied grin to fade into a frown of renewed focus and concentration.

Mary does not remember the final outcome of the bout - but she does remember the lesson. Not everyone plays by the rules. Much like a real-life aggressor, some people will bend the rules and try to win at all costs when the opportunity arises.

In a knife fight, there's no point squealing: "But, *I won*," when someone still intends to attack you. Rules don't count in real combat, because there are no rules.

> **Warriors locked in time**
> **Waiting for a hint of weakness**
> **Lightning flash across the sky**

DAMNED IF YOU DO

WHEN STUDENTS HAVE COMPLETED an evaluation, especially if they feel they have done reasonably well in the evaluation, they are eager to get their results. Those who have not done quite so well tend to prefer to delay the inevitable bad news. Sensei was, you can imagine by now, well attuned to these nuances and used them as part of his personal development arsenal in the dojo.

Jacques and Mary had started the slow and flowing Chinese art of t'ai chi at much the same time, and the bug bit both of them. They trained hard both in class and in extra personal practice and, although they had different strengths and weaknesses, they moved up the ranks consistently together. The pair knew they had both done well (certainly well enough to pass) in their brown sash evaluation and were eagerly awaiting the results.

They'd get keyed up before class, hoping that today would be the day they got their smart new brown sash, but Sensei behaved as though he had forgotten all about the evaluation.

Mary had never liked the blue sash. It was the same colour as her training pants, and she felt it did not stand out enough. She desperately wanted to move up to brown, assuming she had earned it. Unfortunately, quick gratification was not guaranteed in the dojo.

After a couple of classes, the pair asked Sensei if the results were ready, only to be answered with an enigmatic: "Not yet."

The weeks rolled by and Jacques and Mary decided to take it in turns to ask on a weekly basis. Sensei always replied with the same answer, with no indication of when the results would be available nor what was holding them up.

Sensei had been erratic with results in the past. They knew it could take days, or weeks, or even a couple of months, but they still felt that optimistic prickle of hope at the start of each class and the dash of disappointment when nothing was said.

Eventually, Sensei said: "If you stop asking, the results might come out sooner." Well, he said a lot more than that. Sensei had a way of talking around a topic to explain the relevance and nuances before he got to the point - but that was the take home message.

Jacques and Mary stopped asking, and within a couple more weeks they were finally presented with their new sashes. Lesson learned, yet again.

After their black sash evaluation in June or July the next year, Jacques and Mary said nothing. Not a word. The hope still rose and fell in their chests each class like that elusive slow t'ai chi full breath, but they did not bring up the topic once. Not once.

Weeks passed and rolled into months, and months. Jacques and Mary were going to show Sensei that they had mastered the art of going with the flow. They managed to feign total disinterest in the results - although their continued enthusiasm for training was probably enough of a giveaway for Sensei.

Eventually, December arrived. "Are we going to ask?" Mary said to Jacques. "I don't want to go into next year and still not have my results." They agreed that it seemed pointless waiting and decided to ask Sensei.

"Oh," he said. "Your results have been ready for ages. I've been waiting for you to ask. I assumed you were not interested," said Sensei with twinkling eyes and a wide, wicked grin.

Sensei still made them wait a few weeks. They were awarded their black sashes on the very last t'ai chi class of the year, having learned that there are no fixed rules in the dojo. You're damned if you do, and damned if you don't - and losing all ego-attachment to your advancement in the art or unnecessary pride in your belt, grade, or sash, is as important as slow and steady training and progress.

Quite calm motion
Flows dreamily through forms
Energy gathers

A POKER FACE IS
A USEFUL TOOL

PART OF SENSEI'S TRAINING, particularly (but by no means exclusively) in the samurai art of Katori Shinto Ryu, included encouraging students to adopt a poker face. That deadpan inscrutable look that gives away no clues how you are feeling or what you are thinking.

Neil had heard this instruction from Sensei many times, but didn't understand the real value of it, until it was too late.

After several years in the dojo, Neil thought a career in the Navy would suit him well. He duly applied and was accepted on paper. Next up were the physical tests.

Neil did well enough to make it through to the final selection round. The challenges were demanding. Harder than anything Sensei had thrown at him, if that was at all conceivable; physically harder, anyway. But the mental strength Neil had learned from training with Sensei saw him comfortably ready to reach his goal.

The last selection exercise was a time trial against another applicant. Both looked fit and strong, but the tests were tough, and designed to weed out the weakest element. The two in this trial were evenly matched and finished each round more or less at the same time.

On push ups Neil might be ahead by a second, pull ups might see the other applicant ahead ever so slightly. It was going to be photo finish contest. Neil was tired but pushing hard.

His opponent simply matched him, move for move. Speed for speed. Agility and strength all pretty equal. The other contestant seemed to be running effortlessly, like a well-oiled machine that had just reached optimum running temperature.

Last up, on super-tired legs, was a sprint. Neil was starting to think he couldn't match this opponent. Here he was puffing and panting, and the other guy was just cruising - or that's how it appeared from the outside anyway.

The two sprinted hard, Neil pushed himself, but the other guy stayed with him, hardly making a sound. Neil was grunting and gasping for breath until he felt he couldn't beat this guy on the last stretch and slacked off just a little to make it easier on his body.

Neil's opponent crossed the finish line a second or two in the lead and collapsed just after the finish line. Breathing heavily with exhaustion and unable to move without help. It was only then that Neil realised that he had been fooled by his opponent's composed outer appearance.

Neil admitted to Sensei later that, if he'd known how close to collapse his opponent was, he would have found the strength to push a little harder all the way to the finish line. But he gave up before the end because the guy did not appear to be struggling at all.

That was also when Neil understood that the poker face works both ways. His opponent might have given up earlier too, if Neil had not telegraphed his struggle and fatigue.

Courage fails and grows
On an endless journey
The reward – self-growth

GET A GRIP

TRAINING IN THE ART of the sword was a humbling affair for Mary. Some of Sensei's students took to the lessons like ducks to water but Mary stood out like the ugly duckling, waddling about in the shallows while the others were swimming happily in the deep end.

When Mary first started training she used a stock standard, mass-produced, red oak bokken. It arrived in shrink-wrapped crinkly-hard plastic with a gold sticker that probably said: Made in Taiwan. It was on the heavy side, and didn't have the right curvature, but it was affordable and was the initial go to weapon that Sensei stocked for students at the time.

Mary had survived one or two training trips to Holland, and Sensei now had enough students to invite the Dutch Sensei over for a training seminar at our dojo. Mary had more or less gotten the hang of the sword and managed to swim along, duck-like, with the rest - or so she thought - and she was looking forward to the training and learning some new techniques.

For Katori Shinto Ryu the wooden sword training is done without the tsuba or hand guard, but there is a particular way to hold the sword. The leading hand or right hand holds the sword directly behind where the hand guard would be (if it were there). The left or back hand holds the end of the sword with the baby finger half curled off the edge, to stop the sword from slipping in your hands as you thrust into an object.

Mary had spent hours with Sensei training what he called, the eggshell grip. She held the sword firmly, but not too tightly with the baby finger and ring finger holding tighter than the other fingers in the oval shape of an egg. The combination meant you would not drop the egg, but you were also not gripping it so tightly that your wrist was stiff and immobile nor tight enough to break the egg.

To help us perfect this grip, Sensei used to get us to do hours and hours of that rotating strike, maki uchi, with a small coin between our ring finger and the handle, or tsuka, of the sword. If you dropped the coin, you weren't applying enough grip with the smaller two fingers.

Students were also taught that the right hand controlled the direction of the sword, while the left hand was the power or driving hand.

Mary had put in countless hours trying to progress from ugly duckling to duckling stage, so you can imagine her utter dismay when the Dutch Sensei pulled her to one side and proceeded to teach her how to hold the sword.

Some of what he wanted was lost in translation, but Mary went away trying to add his new interpretation. She understood that she was trying to hold the sword like an axe with her right hand, which meant a firm wrist. Once you have ingrained a hard-won habit it is pretty hard to undo it, and Mary spent several unhappy seminar hours trying to relearn how to hold the goddamn weapon she was supposed to wield like a competent war-faring samurai.

A little devil on her shoulder whispered that this doesn't make sense, and contradicts Sensei's training, so Mary decided to ask the Dutch Sensei again for instruction with her Sensei in attendance. Much discussion later Mary was instructed to try and get the webbed vee between her thumb and fingers running in a straight line with the sword.

She tried and failed many times, and had a frustrating seminar spent focused on, yet failing to master, this new sword grip. It was only towards the very end of the seminar that poor Mary started to realise that she had been set an impossible task. She is shorter than average. Her hands are smaller than average, and the sword handle was simply too large for her hand. There was no way she could hold the sword handle correctly in all places at once, with fingers curved around the oval and that elusive vee on top.

At that point, Mary was able to get a grip on the problem and realised that a one-size-fits-all solution does not actually work for all students in the dojo. One of Sensei's students had started to make handmade bokken and Mary commissioned one more suited to her hand size - and her grip problem was solved immediately.

Mary encountered a similar issue when she started to learn the naginata syllabus. The naginata is similar to a medieval glaive - imagine a long pole with a sword or large blade attached to the end of it. All naginata have oval handles, but the handle of Mary's first handmade naginata was round instead of oval.

Usually, one edge of the oval shape was lined up with the

naginata blade so you knew where the blade was pointing by touch. Except for the ugly duckling, called Mary, with a round naginata who had no guide to blade direction other than stopping to glance at it, and was constantly being corrected by Sensei.

Again when we moved to the o' naginata or large naginata, Sensei would insist that Mary hold the naginata with her right hand at shoulder height when the ishi tsuki or butt of the naginata was on the floor. If she did that with the o' naginata the blade would impale itself in the group on some of the circular moves required of the weapon.

Mary would drop on one knee and slice menacingly at her opponent's leg. The opponent would move adeptly out the way and go for Mary's exposed head. At this point, most students would elegantly stand up and use the butt end of the naginata to effortless sweep the attacking sword out the way. All expect the ugly duckling, Mary, would impale the long end with the blade into the ground while trying to swing the blade passed her body to bring the butt into play.

Simply put, for someone Mary's height she needed a different hand position (right hand at eye height) to use the weapon effectively.

Mary only managed to convince Sensei of this when she showed him a video of a similarly short Japanese lady wielding the naginata using that grip. Up until then, Mary suspects Sensei thought she was simply still an ugly duckling. In many ways, she still was. But she did get a grip on that one-size-fits-all thing, and now knows it only works for Joe Average.

Oh - and if you're wondering. No, Mary didn't learn any new techniques in the seminar with the Dutch Sensei. But she did learn to trust her judgement, to question supposedly immutable training rules, and it helped Mary to be more compassionate with her own students when the time came.

Glinting sharp sword tip
Draws the eye to the hidden
Spring laughter cut short

THE DELUGE

SENSEI WAS ALWAYS LOOKING for new ways to stay fit and challenge his students. At one point, he decided that the students could do with more cardiovascular fitness and running became the order of the day. There was never enough time for all the training that needed to be done, so Sensei invited Edmund to runs in addition to his normal training.

Like most things, Sensei approached the topic with seriousness and careful preparation. Edmund was convinced Sensei visited and ran with ALL the various running clubs in town with the express purpose of uncovering the most unreasonable and intimidating running crew available.

Sensei eventually settled on the Harriers running club with a mix of great runners over all distances.

A date was announced for some of Sensei's gang of students to meet for an inaugural run with the Harriers.

Like most extra activities that Sensei arranged, the hour was early. Very early. For extra effect, the weather was howling and wet. There was a long downpour of cataclysmic proportions. Council crews were sandbagging the beaches, sewers and drains were overflowing, and riverside roads were waterlogged and closed off.

Sensei's crowd turned up at the appointed petrol station at the appointed early hour and stood in the deluge, chatting and stretching ahead of the much-anticipated run.

The weather was so bad that not one single member of the Harriers arrived for their regular Saturday morning run.

Needless to say, Edmund enjoyed a run with Sensei and company heading across the bridge and down onto the beachfront, following the beach road and back again.

"That day I realised how special the training I was receiving truly was," said Edmund. "The thing is, the possibility of not turning up for the run didn't cross one of our minds. We decided to do it, so we did it - nothing special.

"The facts on the ground (and falling voluminously from the sky) really didn't enter into it. What mattered were the facts in our mind and the commitments made. To this day I drive my wife batty by going running in snow and sloshing mud, because that day I learned that what happens inside my head wins out over whatever happens outside," said Edmund.

Of course, Sensei's gang were feeling a little superior for having turned up in the deluge second only to Noah's, but those thoughts quickly vanished the next appointed run morning when the Harriers left Sensei's determined but plodding students behind in a spectacle of antelope-like grace and speed... which was, of course, the point.

Delicate fragrance
Wafts lightly into the hall
Pink carpet of blossoms

SUSPENDING COMMON SENSE

OUR DOJO WAS APPROACHED to provide sword demonstrations, even paid performances, from time to time, but Sensei usually refused for one principled reason or another. So when Sensei announced that we would be doing performances at several movie theatres in prominent malls to promote the launch of Tom Cruise in The Last Samurai, we were simultaneously surprised and excited.

Performing in front of a crowd had its own interesting challenges. Mary worked through trying to look cool, calm, and collected doing t'ai chi on jelly legs. There had been occasions where she'd fervently hoped that people would interpret the visible shaking as her pulsating aura and energy field as opposed to the nervous energy that it was. So she knew this round of demonstrations would present its own unique set of challenges.

Surprisingly, the events went off without too much drama. Especially for a demo crew doing one-to-two demos a day, every evening after work for several weeks, with a couple more on the weekends. It was hard work, but we approached it as valuable extra training - which it was.

Fortunately, performing at speed under pressure is easier than moving at t'ai chi snail's pace. So all it took was gently coaxing those flighty butterflies into rough formation - enough to start - and the speed and immediacy of the katas, ingrained with countless repetitions, did the rest.

By the third week, our performances were widely anticipated by the mall staff, and many timed their toilet and smoke breaks to catch us in action. And that's where the rumours of legends started.

It wasn't too long before a spectator, with tongue firmly in cheek, told someone else how we flew down to the movie theatre area without using the elevators. In fertile and susceptible minds we became the real life ninjas - the stuff of movies. Only wearing navy hakama (pleated pants worn by the samurai) instead of an all-black outfit.

The idea took hold and the stories circulated through the spectators, getting wilder and more implausible with each retelling as nuances and super powers were added each time. We had fellow students in the audience who would chuckle with amusement or add an embellishment of their own.

Mary was both relieved (it had been a long, tiring stint) and sad to hand in her superhero status at the end of the demonstrations. How boring to become a normal human again!

Sensei took us to an ice-cream parlour as a celebration, with all of us still dressed in our training gear and dragging sheathed weapons of various shapes and sizes around with us. As Mary ordered her favourite caramel crunch, with an impossible-to-pronounce fancy Italian name, the lady serving her stared wide-eyed, as though she was seeing a ghost or a battle-hardened samurai back from the dead.

She eventually plucked up enough courage.

"Is it true that you guys can float down from, like, the top floor?" she asked.

Clearly part of her wanted to get caught up in the glorious fantasy of it all, while part of her was thinking: is this really possible?

Mary hesitated for a moment. It was mildly tempting to lead someone along, if they were willing to suspend their common sense and buy into fantastical tales, but she had always had a black and white view of truth. Mary gently said no and watched the lady blush for a second before handing over my ice-cream cup.

It was then that Mary started to understand how the origins of arts become the stories of legends as opposed to hard facts.

Patience, the victor
Emerges like soft violets from
The ruins of your mind

THE WEIGHTY MATTER OF EGO

MARY WAS QUIETLY PLEASED with her progress. She had been learning t'ai chi with Sensei for a couple of years now and was close to knowing all three sections of the Yang long form, which she felt was a fairly impressive achievement with a demanding teacher like Sensei.

She moved confidently. She practised every day, and Mary felt she'd almost mastered t'ai chi. She directed her movement from the ground via the hips and took great pride in the leg strength she had developed and the ease and grace with which she performed the movements.

Sensei paid close attention to his students and their energy and attitude when training. It wasn't long after Mary's confidence blossomed that she found herself training section one ad nauseam with the beginners - except she had the pleasure of sporting ugly neoprene ankle weights that made it difficult to bend her ankles. Sometimes, she also had velcro wrist weights cutting off the circulation to her hands to add to her list of class miseries.

To make matters worse, Sensei was teaching the very end of section three to the rest of the more advanced students and Mary was not included.

Training with Sensei has one of those uncomfortable conundrums. You sign up for training to learn self-defence, a martial art, or t'ai chi - but the reality of training with Sensei is that you are signing up to learn about yourself and discover a myriad of ways to challenge your limits, and your ego, every step of the way. Even something like the graceful art of t'ai chi hides some subtle combat and life lessons.

At first, Mary thought it was one of Sensei's erratic whims. She assumed it was a one-off thing to show her that she really had a long way to go to in the leg strength department. She also assumed that Sensei only had one set of weights and it would be someone else's turn to sport the weight for the next class. Then she assumed it would last a week - or maybe two.

As the week evolved into weeks, and weeks, Mary became progressively more and more annoyed with Sensei. She felt he was holding her back; that he was being unfair and favouring the other students. She seethed and fumed her way through classes - the antithesis of the calm and controlled expression she was supposed to portray, until she finally exhausted her anger and started to focus on the form.

Mary began to realise that just wearing the weights changed her centre and balance and produced a strong sense of rootedness. She began to experiment at home, without the weights, trying to recreate that feeling of connectedness to the ground.

She also realised that her steps and kicks were so much

easier without the weights on and that she moved with more control and precision than ever before. And finally, when she let go of the weighty matter of ego she realised the full potential of the lesson; one part humility, one part physical strength, and a new way to focus on and improve her moves.

Stroke of misfortune
Leaves a battling hollow self
A stranger's kind smile

WRINGING THE CLOTH

THE LAST SAMURAI MOVIE did a lot to drive interest in learning the samurai arts. It added a certain glamour and Hollywood flavour to sword training, as movies tend to do - and it brought on a surge in student enrolments. Each new potential student attracted by their own interpretation of the power and allure of the art of the sword and its possible physical, mental, and more esoteric benefits.

Entering a traditional dojo came as quite a shock to some of these students, suddenly confronted with unusual requirements such as cleaning the dojo floor before and after training.

You could see Western-influenced commercial indignation flash across potential student's faces when Sensei introduced the concept. Some were quick to bristle with a look that clearly said: I'm paying for classes - not to be your skivvy - and I'm certainly not paying for the privilege of cleaning your training floor. Others bought into the concept for a while and then had a delayed: "Woah, I somehow signed up for a cleaning job," type of reaction.

But, if they wanted to train, they had to clean the floor.

The dojo is a great ego-challenger and as the saying goes: Even a master steps into his hakama one leg at a time. With Sensei, there was no escape from showing respect for the training area and your fellow classmates by helping to clean the dojo floor.

As with everything else in Sensei's dojo, there was a particular way to clean the floor, and it was designed to improve training as well. A hint of Mr Miyagi's wipe on, wipe off training as shown in The Karate Kid.

It was also designed to test a student's commitment and determination. If a student couldn't lower himself to the clean the floor as instructed he, or she, was not going to last long in Sensei's class. So it was no bother to Sensei if the requirement created personal angst and soul-searching in some or put other potential students off altogether.

Cotton towelling or other cotton cloths were soaked in a bucket of cold water. The most junior students had the task of wringing out the water and passing the cloths to the other students. They would place each cloth on the ground, roughly shoulder-width apart, with their hands pressing the edges of the cloth to the floor.

Forming a line, shoulder to shoulder, the students would push off with their legs, running the cloth across the floor in a peculiar crunched push-up position. When they got practised at it, the students were literally running while pushing their cloths across the floor, and it was quite an exhilarating, if head throbbing, warm up.

After reaching the edge of the dojo, each student would turn around, pick another line to wipe clean and head back across the dojo floor. The cloth was then plunked back (often with a celebratory splash) into the bucket to soak, while the poor cloth-wringing and splash-drenched junior students rinsed a new cloth, wrung it out, and supplied fresh cleaning material.

In winter, the largely sedentary cold-water cloth wringing was by far the least desired job, and it obviously fell to the most junior students of each class to freeze their fingers to the bone.

Sensei would teach the students to hold the folded cloth as though they were holding a sword handle - one hand above the other, palms facing in. To squeeze out the water the students had to rotate both thumbs inward in a wringing motion that mimicked the correct and strongest grip on a sword. The elbows were to be pulled in and the armpits slightly closed.

Not an easy feat to master when trying to keep on top of Sensei's list of requirements and meet the endless demand for floor cloths - and every beginner's prayer was the fervent hope that someone new would sign up soon.

Quiet heart
Empty mind
At ease with how the world unfolds

THE EARLY BIRD

SENSEI WAS A STICKLER for punctuality, at least for the start of class. Most classes tended to end when they finished, which was often well after the official end time, but they always started on time - always. Even if Sensei was delayed or busy, the most senior student would automatically ask the class to line up, bow in and the class would begin.

Students were repeatedly told to "take ten off" and aim to arrive ten minutes early, so they were ready and on the floor at the start of class. Most students learnt to do this quickly, but Sean stood out as an exception.

Early mornings and Sean were not exactly on speaking terms. He would arrive as the class was called to line up, hair still tousled, pulling on the last half of his gi, while trying to run along the corridor and stumble into the dojo - and that was on a good day.

As winter approached and morning training became harder, Sean got progressively later. For a while he got away with a breathless: "Sorry I'm late, Sensei," as he rubbed at his eyes, stifled a yawn, pulled at the knot of his belt and stepped onto the dojo floor.

But as the cold of winter set in Sean got later and later. On one bitterly cold and dark morning, Sean arrived 15 minutes late expecting to be allowed onto the floor. He was met by an angry Sensei who told him to stay outside and train until called for.

Half an hour later, after checking several times to make sure that Sean was in fact training, Sensei invited Sean into the warmth of the dojo, and we all sat through yet another lecture for Sean's benefit. A lecture about the importance and value of respect; respect for the teacher, fellow students, classmates, and oneself. It was also a lecture about sticking to your word and doing what you said you would do; and about the importance of being on time - for work, for friends, for life partners...

Sean was on time for the next class, but it was a hard lesson for him to learn. Come time for the next class, and he was late again - and sent to train outside, again.

Sensei left him to train outside in the cold for even longer this time. Sean was called onto the dojo floor one hour into the 90-minute class, and we all listened to another lecture.

The next class, Sean didn't arrive at all.

We heard from Sensei that Sean had called later that morning to say he had slept through his alarm.

The following class, Sean arrived late again, to find the dojo door locked. He went to train on his own outside - which he did for the full 90-plus minutes as Sensei decided not to invite him to join the class.

Not too long after that Sean started to arrive a few minutes early for class, like everyone else. Lesson learnt, perhaps, but it did happen to coincide with the days getting warmer and the mornings being lighter.

The cold quiet
Before dawn
We bow and train

WHAT'S THE APPLICATION?

ONE OF SENSEI'S FORTES was the ability to remember and demonstrate a range of self-defence applications for the moves in kata he taught. It was something he enjoyed and a highlight of the class for the students - except for the hapless student who was selected as Sensei's demonstration partner.

In fact, the students enjoyed watching the applications in action so much that they would often try to distract Sensei by asking him to show and demonstrate the moves. As a new student, Edmund had caught onto this and was silly enough to ask the application of some of the wrist movements down during the warm up.

Sensei always encouraged his new students to experience the techniques, so when he called for a volunteer, Edmund was first up and eagerly anticipating the first-hand lesson will all the innocence and trusting enthusiasm of a kid let loose in the playground.

"Right. These exercises are all different types of wrist locks.

Grab my wrist with your left hand," instructed Sensei as he extended his left arm for the grab.

Edmund obligingly grabbed with his right hand.

"The *other* left hand," roared Sensei. "I want a cross grab for this technique."

Edmund smiled foolishly and grabbed Sensei's left wrist with his left hand.

"That's better," said Sensei as he deftly trapped Edmund's fingers against his arm and executed a neat nikyo that saw Edmund drop instantly onto one knee and tap sharply on his leg three times to let Sensei know to ease off the pressure.

"Wow, that was neat. Can we do it again," asked Edmund, wanting to figure out how it worked.

"Oh we will," said Sensei with his wicked grin, as he went on to demonstrate nikyo at a slightly slower and noticeably more excruciatingly painful pace.

With Edmund still as his demo partner, Sensei then broke down nikyo into teaching steps. With each repetition, Edmund's wrist became more sensitive and reactive until he was pre-empting the technique and dropping to his knees before Sensei had applied the lock.

"I'll pay you $10 after class," joked Sensei as he always did when someone made the technique look more effective than it was, "but wait until I've actually applied the technique, okay!"

"Yes, Sensei," said Edmund rubbing his wrist and standing up a lot slower than necessary to stall for recovery time.

Sensei showed the class again in slow motion. Using his right palm Sensei pressed hard against Edmund's fingers, trapping Edmund's hand in the grab position. Sensei then lifted his left fingers skyward and dove them down sharply toward the ground, in what he called a dolphin dive. The pressure on Edmund's wrist had him on his knees again, tapping out.

"Grab a partner and practice," said Sensei who moved around the dojo correcting here, helping there. After a few minutes, Sensei declared it was time for the next technique: kote gaeshi.

Edmund, now a little wiser, wasn't about to volunteer his services as a demonstration partner again. It was far more enjoyable watching Sensei than being on the receiving end of his techniques. Sensei caught Edmund's eye. Edmund tried to look away but heard: "Edmund, come. We need to balance out the pain."

This time, Sensei grabbed Edmund's right hand. He got his vice-like fingers around the base of Edmund's thumb and had his thumb pressing against the knuckle of the little finger, turning outwards and downwards, neatly dropping Edmund, who was not yet trained in the Aikido roll, into an untidy bundle on the floor.

Unperturbed
The warrior stands on guard
Alone in the dancing moonlight

CORRECT THE MISTAKE

MONTY WAS STRUGGLING ALONG gamely in class when Sensei introduced swari gedan. Much to the dismay of Monty's creaking old knees (although Monty was, in fact, younger than Sensei) swari gedan required what Monty called a hoppity-skip back, followed by inadvertently banging one knee on the ground while dropping into a one-knee crouch. It also involved simultaneously lowering the sword in front of the body with the kisage glinting towards the floor in the dim early morning dojo light.

The first part of the class involved getting that one knee crouch correct.

"Stand with your right leg in front, in a normal forward stance. Good," said Sensei glancing around the class. "Now drop your left knee to the ground. No, keep your toes bent. Monty! Curl your toes under so you can stand up again quickly if you need to without adjusting the foot."

"Now keep upright. Don't lower your bum to the ground,

keep your hips up and back up straight. This is a taunting and luring posture. You want to keep your head high as a tempting target and then cut your opponent from underneath," said Sensei.

Apart from the reverberating clunk when Monty's knee hit the oak floorboards harder than it ought to, this part of training went quite quickly.

"Now, grab your bokuto," said Sensei as he showed the class how to move from a forward stance, with the kisage threatening the opponent's eyes. Monty watched as Sensei lowered the sword to ankle height and floated effortlessly and silently towards the floor in a synchronised and elegant crouch.

Monty blinked and shook his head. The graceful move already lost in a blur of confusion.

"Swari gedan," called Sensei. The class moved in unison into the new crouch position. Everyone had their body straight, toes under, sword lowered - except Monty.

"Drop onto your back knee Monty, and lower your sword point," said Sensei breaking the move down for Monty. "Now keep your sword point forward along your midline to provide the best protection and show that you are in control."

After a few repetitions, Monty was able to drop to one knee and stand up again - not elegantly, but smoothly enough for Sensei to overlook the smaller errors and wavering sword, for now.

"Now we're going to add the sugi ashi," said Sensei, doing a little the hoppity-skip shuffle backwards before dropping into swari gedan.

"It's a quick shuffle out the way of an attack, but I'll break it down. You start with your right foot in front in a forward stance. Now bring that right foot back to your left foot, and then you send the left leg back, so you end up in the same stance as before - just further back," explained Sensei.

"So front foot back, back foot back. Let's go. Ichi," said Sensei, starting the count for ten sugi ashi.

Everyone pulled their right foot to their left and sent their left leg back - even Monty, although he was a bit slower and kept checking what other people were doing to see if he had got it right.

Monty made it to ju without an error, so Sensei said: "Good, now let's combine this with the drop onto the knee. Ichi..."

Monty did the sugi ashi shuffle, but then pulled his right leg back again as he started to kneel and fell forward putting a hand out just before he kissed the freshly washed floorboards.

"Again, but stop after the sugi ashi," said Sensei. Monty repeated his new version of the shuffle, ending with his feet together, without a wide and stable base to lower his body. He stood and scratched his head.

"Monty, you've pulled your right leg back. You should be in a normal forward stance," said Sensei.

Monty stepped his left leg back to end up in a forward stance.

"No," roared Sensei. "You'll never learn if you correct the leg that didn't make a mistake."

Monty was visibly flustered. He was in a forward stance like the other students and had no idea what he had done wrong.

"Let's try again," said Sensei.

The class did a perfect sugi ashi, except for poor Monty. He did the sugi ashi and pulled his right leg back again.

"Monty," said Sensei, trying hard not to sound exasperated.

Monty looked wildly around the class and cautiously stepped his left leg back so that he was in a forward stance like everyone else.

"No, Monty. You did a sugi ashi and then this," said Sensei, pulling his right leg back to the left. "That naughty right leg of yours should have stayed in front - so to correct the mistake, your right leg needs to go forward, not the left leg back. It wouldn't be appropriate for me to correct Mary when you made a mistake, now would it? So you need to correct the leg that made the mistake."

"One more time," said Sensei.

Monty did his hoppity-skip. The right leg pulled half way back and faltered. Monty's left leg twitched, but then he caught it and sent the right leg back to where it should have been.

"Now everybody, drop into swari gedan," said Sensei.

Dawn light exposes
The nature of things
Shut up and train harder

CHEESHI CHEAT

ONE DAY, EDMUND ARRIVED at class to see Sensei busily cutting broomstick handles into thirds. Curious, thought Edmund, as he eyed a motley range of jam tins and plastic flowerpots in a haphazard row next to the growing pile of sticks.

"I wonder what new delights of torture Sensei has in store for us," he mused.

Towards the end of class, each student was given a sawn-off piece of broomstick handle, a tin or flowerpot, and some nails. The mission was to hammer the nails sideway into the bottom portion of the stick and to plant the stick in the flowerpot or tin -nail side down like plant roots- into a mixture of concrete, which was to be poured in and left to cure.

Sensei's students dutifully returned to the next class with their homework complete, proudly carrying their broom handle pieces firmly cemented into the flowerpots and tins.

These new instruments of torture were assorted sizes, and now that they were filled with concrete it was clear they were assorted weights.

Edmund noted that his pot was mid-sized and that Sensei's live-in students or deshi had been allocated the largest pots Sensei had managed to source. He wondered what on earth they were for, but was no longer foolish enough to ask. He knew he would find out soon enough, and that he would probably be sorry once he knew.

Edmund, being both curious and practical, had secretly weighed his concrete flowerpot contraption. It was just over 2.5kgs. He figured the deshi's concrete flowerpots must be close to 5kgs.

"Pick up your cheeshi, grab a mat, and line up," called out Sensei.

It didn't take too much intelligence to figure out that the new cement weights on sticks must be called cheeshi - and everyone grabbed theirs along with a mat and lined up.

"Put your mat down in front of you, and put your cheeshi on the mat. I don't want you to damage the wooden floor," said Sensei.

He proceeded to show the class how to use the cheeshi.

"Turn your right hand upside down like this," said Sensei as he moved to what looked like a thumbs down sign, "and grab the top of the stick while you drop down into shiko. Good.

"Now swing the cheeshi in an arc to above your head so that the cement head is balanced above the stick you have in your hand, like holding a lollipop. Now lower your right hand slowly in front of you, with the arm extended, and stop at shoulder height," said Sensei.

Edmund let out a quiet, "Phew." Something about the

physics of having the weight at the end of the stick, at the furthest point from his hand, made this a lot harder than just picking up 2.5kgs.

"Now return the cheeshi to your mat, following the path you used to get it there. Lift up, turn it over, and place it gently on the mat, concrete side down."

After several repetitions with both hands, Sensei added the next move. Once everyone had their cheeshi extended in front of their shoulder, he said, "Now, keeping your arm extended, lift the cheeshi up and then, bending at the elbow, lower it down your back. No! Stay in shiko. Lower. You should be able to balance a teacup on those thighs."

"Now, straighten your arm above your head and lower the cheeshi slowly back in front of your shoulder," said Sensei.

Every class, the dreaded cheeshi came out and Sensei added a new move, a swing between the legs that reminded Edmund of kettle bell work, and a twirling movement, rotating the cheeshi to the side and around over the shoulder and forward. That one really tested Edmund's wrist strength.

When the class had finally learnt the complete set of cheeshi exercises, Sensei decided it was time to increase the challenge by increasing the weight.

"Everybody grab a heavier cheeshi," ordered Sensei. "Deshi Tony, bring me your cheeshi."

Tony paled and took on a sickly pallor.

"Rory's cheeshi is heavier, Sensei. C-c-ca -can I bring you that one," stammered Tony.

Sensei strode over and picked up Tony's cheeshi, expecting a good 5kgs of resistance. But it flew skyward with the weight of a feather. Well, the weight of a flowerpot, wood, nails and concrete-coloured polystyrene to be exact.

"Interesting, Tony," said Sensei in a controlled but loud

whisper, alarmingly at odds with his angry demeanour. "Tony, grab Rory's cheeshi and stand in front of the class. I think your training for this evening is cheeshi until lights out."

Being one of Sensei's live-in students, Tony had no way to escape his lesson, and his polystyrene-trained arms did cheeshi with 5kgs for hours on end.

Eyes locked across the dojo
The Sensei and the student
A cold shiver before dawn

THE 100-DAY GONG

MARY HAD OFTEN HEARD Sensei say that it takes between 100 and 1,000 days to entrench a good habit, but she was sceptical when Sensei decided to add a practical slant and introduce a 100-day gong. The idea was that each student would pick something beneficial to do, and commit to doing it for 100 days.

It could be anything. Press-ups to improve arm strength, a daily set of t'ai chi. "It could even be brushing your teeth every morning, if that is something you don't usually do," said Sensei.

Mary decided to watch the other students for a while, to see how it all worked.

Sensei's selected gong was to do 1,000 wrist turns holding his naginata out in front of him, to improve his forearm strength and grip. He had always found challenges to be a great motivator. Sensei also decided that his students should keep him company for his gong, so most of the students in his classes were exhorted to join in, using bo if they did not have a naginata; Mary was one of them.

For the first 21 days or so, Sensei's gong progressed nicely. There was one occasion when he almost forgot and had to get out of bed to do the 1,000 wrist turns. But all was on track, and about 15 minutes of Mary's class time was consumed with the mind numbing rolling of the naginata.

"Character-building stuff," Sensei would say as they went forwards for 100 turns, backwards for 100 turns, and then changed the naginata around so that the heavier blade end was on the other side of the body. One hundred forward, 100 back.

Mary's dislike for gongs increased with each encounter. She discovered that her forearms muscles could scream with pain but could keep on working, and working. She also discovered, to her extreme dismay, that if Sensei accidentally missed a day, the gong began all over again from zero.

Sensei forgot to do his gong on day 59, just when Mary was starting to see an end to the regular class torture session. And then Sensei forgot again on day seven. And again not long after that.

Progress for all of Sensei's students was like that. Their gongs were an on-going round of recounts.

Mary hated gongs *so* much that she decided she was going to show everybody how to do it right. One of her favourite mottos was: Get it right the first time - and she was determined to show everyone how that was done.

To help her succeed, Mary picked a gong she considered difficult. Something that she would really not want to do for one single day more than was necessary. She picked 100 kneeling strikes with the bo. This required striking down towards an opponent's foot or ankle while dropping to the ground, standing up while loading the bo behind her, alternating legs and striking down again. One. Hundred. Times.

Sensei smiled with encouragement when Mary told him she was finally doing a gong to show the rest of them how to do it properly. He sometimes even invited the class to join her for her daily gong. The rest of the class did not think much of her plan and suffered through it much like they did with Sensei's wrist turns.

Mary battled through though days with headaches and good days when the gong was fun. She never missed a day - not once. She felt proud of her achievement and the fact that Sensei was able to ride the wave of her determination and also completed his gong - which meant a temporary end to the regular class torture of gongs.

The next time the subject of gongs came up at the dojo, Mary decided to do a particular set of qigong moves for 100 days. She had good days and bad days, and days when, like Sensei, she had to get out of bed to do her gong before midnight. She did her qigong set in airport toilets and hotel rooms, and eventually missed a day or two on the way and had to start again.

That, of course, was the real lesson. To try and keep trying, even when you failed once, or twice, or more often. Everyone can do something for 100 days; not everyone can keep going and restart from zero when they miss a day.

Incidentally, Sensei's record for the longest time to complete a gong - which happened to be 100 squats for 100 days - took just over a year to complete. Many students had the pleasure of joining him on the journey of that gong.

In seiza
Lost in meditation
The bell bird calls

THE LAST CLASS
OF THE YEAR

HAVING SURVIVED HIS FIRST end of year training class the previous year, Edmund smiled knowingly, almost with fond nostalgia, when Sensei announced the upcoming special year-end combined training class.

He figured he knew what to expect, and with typical Edmund overzealousness, he was even looking forward to the physical and mental test. Wondering how much easier 2000, plus one, punches would be this year on top of all his training.

When the day arrived Edmund was secretly pleased to find and check the counting marker weapons around the dojo. He was chatting amiably on the floor while warming up when Sensei walked into the dojo.

"Yoi," said Sensei, calling everyone to attention.

The students shuffled apprehensively into line and bowed

when the most senior student called a sharp: "Sensei, ni rei."

This year, everyone was asked to form a circle. Sensei moved students around the perimeter circle, mixing grade levels, so there was a senior student, then a junior student, senior, junior, and so on.

"Stepping forward, into right leg zenkutsu dachi, with chudan no kamae," said Sensei. Everyone stepped right leg forward and brought their fists up to the chest level on guard position.

"Left leg maegeri. Ichi. Ni. San..." said Sensei, counting up to ten while executing crisp textbook-perfect forward kicks. He continued to count to one hundred.

"Change legs and right leg maegeri," said Sensei, as he broke out into another round of ichi to hyaku.

After the initial surprise at discovering that the end of year class meant thousands of any one particular technique that took Sensei's fancy rather than the assumed chest punches executed last year, Edmund's mind was busy.

He calculated that his legs were considerably heavier than his arms, so it was a no-brainer that this was going to be physically harder than last year.

But his legs were more used to carrying his weight, so perhaps the exercise was equivalent? There again a snapping front kick was supposed to be to the height of the knot in his belt, and his legs soon told him that they were not really used to doing hundreds upon hundreds of those.

"Gohyaku," Sensei called out loudly. The clatter of another weapon on the dojo floor crashed through Edmund's train of thought and brought him back to the moment and legs that were threatening to break ranks and rebel.

Edmund glanced around him at the sea of sweaty faces, most with frowns of concentration, a couple with maniacal grins, or was it well-camouflaged grimaces?

The beginners' kicks had lost their snap, just dropping uncontrolled to the floor. At least half the class was kicking well below waist height, but their legs were moving, and they were trying - and that was the point.

When any of them flagged or showed signs of stopping a nearby senior would drop a word or encouragement, or kiai louder, and the combined energy of the class carried them through to the next count of 100.

Edmund hit his own personal lows, forcing himself to the end of the one-hundred with a false promise of taking a break if he only got that far. At 100, he changed legs, so there was a little strength remaining to start again. Besides, how could he stop and give up with the rest of the dojo watching?

"Ah, another of the many manifold secrets of Sensei's strange ways," thought Edmund as he pushed on, through pain and trembling legs. Trying intermittently to produce a good technique, but mostly just willing himself to keep moving and keep standing.

Letting go
This too will pass
Dew drops on the grass

THE MEMBERSHIP BOOK

RICHARD WAS NERVOUS ABOUT his evaluation. His anticipation had built ever up since Sensei had put his name down for the evaluation a few weeks ago. It reached a crescendo of panic when he had written down the grading requirements by hand - something Sensei insisted must be done that way and not just handed out as printouts.

Richard went home and ticked off the moves he knew. There were long sections with no ticks, and that is when Richard started to panic. He was tempted to ask Sensei if he could postpone his evaluation, but that was tricky ground. If Sensei put your name forward for an evaluation he either considered you ready for the next level - or in need of a kick in the pants to get you to the next level.

Realising he was in the dojo equivalent of being between a proverbial rock and a hard place, Richard did the next best thing and gave Sensei a list of moves he needed to be taught and started practising like crazy.

When the day arrived, Richard reckoned he had a 50:50 chance of passing his evaluation and a slightly better chance of getting a regrade, which would mean repeating the few techniques he blew out on at the evaluation the following month. His anxiety levels were high and Richard wasn't thinking about what he needed to bring with him to the dojo or for the evaluation.

Richard arrived early so he could find a quiet place to relax and centre himself before it was time to enter the dojo.

"Ah, Richard! You're nice and early," greeted Sensei. "Bring your membership book through as soon as you are ready."

"Morning, Sensei,' said Richard, a look of panic crossing his face. Membership book? Of course, he needed to hand in his membership book - but it was at home.

"Err... I forgot my membership book, Sensei," Richard blurted out in horror.

"Then you'd better go home and fetch it - and make sure you are back in time. Evaluations, just like opportunities in life, don't wait for late comers," said Sensei.

Richard had arrived 30 minutes early, but it was a 20-minute drive home and another 20 back. Plus, he had no idea which safe hiding place his membership book was lurking in.

Cursing, Richard was tempted just to give up, but he knew Sensei would disapprove of that. He had to try, even if he didn't come back in time - he had to be seen to try.

Richard phoned home as he got in the car. He asked his mother to look for his membership book and to meet him at a supermarket halfway home if she found it. Just as Richard was passing the supermarket he received a text that his mother was on the way.

He gave his mother a hurried hug, grabbed the membership book and headed back to the dojo. He had saved a few minutes, but probably not enough to get past Sensei.

Richard parked hard, tearing at the lawn in a way that would annoy Sensei if he were to notice, and sprinted from the car park to the dojo, up the stairs, and along the veranda. He got to the door just as Sensei said: "Everybody line up."

Richard continued up to the evaluation table.

"Here's my membership book, Sensei," he said, handing over the book with adrenalin-charged hands.

"Well done, Richard. Now go and... Wait. Before you line up where is your belt?"

Richard looked down. In his anxiety, he had completely forgotten his belt too.

"I... I...," stammered Richard.

"Someone lend Richard a belt. You know you're not allowed on the dojo floor without a belt," said Sensei.

A white belt student quickly untied their belt knot, whipped it off their waist and offered it to Richard with two hands. Richard accepted it gratefully with a bow and hurriedly wound it around his waist and through the belt loops.

Tying the knot as he stepped into line, Richard was already sweating with his right leg twitching nervously. Sensei started with the basic moves, which allowed Richard some time to regain his composure.

A few minutes into the evaluation, Sean ran up to the dojo, his weapons clattering noisily against each other in his denim-blue weapons bag.

"Tahmid Sensei, go and see what Sean wants. If he has arrived late for his evaluation, send him home. It is like arriving late for a job interview - a total waste of time," said Sensei.

Sean was sent home, but Richard went on to pass his

evaluation - just well enough to avoid that feared regrade.

Challenges stretch your
Comfort zones to near breaking
Epiphany – you survive

Challenges stretch your
Comfort zones to near breaking
Epiphany – you survive

NOW GIVE ME MIRROR IMAGE

SIMON WAS IN SERIOUS training mode for his next evaluation. He popped into the dojo every day before class to put in extra practice. He worked hard, focusing on a sword kata. Watching his reflection in the mirror until he was happy with what he saw.

After a couple of weeks, Simon felt he had perfected the sequence and the timing of the kata and was quietly brimming with confidence. He even joked that he had trained so hard that his trusty red oak bokken had the sequence ingrained into it and could do the kata on its own without his input.

On one of his last practice sessions before the evaluation Simon arrived early as usual to practice in front of the dojo mirrors. He heard Sensei's voice and then the dojo door opened quietly and Simon realised that Sensei was standing at the door, watching.

The kata went as planned and Simon, mildly aware that he was showing off, thought to himself, "Nailed that one." The dojo door whispered shut again, and Simon felt a swelling of pride in his effort.

On the day of the evaluation Simon was called onto the dojo floor, along with three other students, to perform the sword kata. Each student was asked to face a different direction to eliminate the possibility of any copying or cheating.

Facing a different direction can also create a sense of disorientation and was a standard test that Sensei used to see how well students knew a particular kata sequence.

Simon was placed facing the evaluation panel, and with a little bit of arrogance that comes with hard work and practice he was confident that he had this one in the bag.

With a loud: "Hajime," Sensei gave the instruction to begin, but as Simon was about to draw his trusty bokken, he added, "Simon, give me mirror image."

Simon blinked and swallowed hard. "Mirror image, Sensei?" he muttered.

"Yes, Simon. Do the kata on the left-hand side, holding the sword in your left hand."

Simon's mind was reeling. He briefly considered arguing the point. Sensei had always maintained there were no left-handed swordsmen, as that brought the heart closer to the opponent's weapon.

Simon took a deep breath and changed hands. He fumbled badly through the kata, with painful pauses and obvious errors, on the left-hand side to produce a mirror image of the kata he had ingrained so well - but not well enough.

Dejected, Simon bowed out after the kata having swallowed another lesson in pride and dojo humility.

The mirror gives off
Distorted reflections of self
You are more than you seem

NOTHING INTERRUPTS TRAINING

THE GENERAL RULE INSIDE the dojo - and when training outside - is that nothing interrupts training. Not phone calls or text messages; not even medical emergencies. Training always continued. Emergencies were dealt with, but training continued either under Sensei or under a senior student.

On one particular summer gasshuku, at a picturesque campsite in the mountains, Sensei had about 40 students lined up, running through some punching drills. It had been a glorious sultry summer day and everyone was trying to kiai louder than the deafening cicada chorus from the nearby trees.

The lighting changed a little, and a slight breeze picked up, prompting Jeremy to glance skywards while trying to keep to Sensei's count. He caught a glimpse of a thick bank of angry black clouds approaching, promising an impressive afternoon thunderstorm.

Jeremy kept a wary eye on the clouds, as Sensei kept the

class going, despite the approaching claps of thunder echoing off the mountains away in the distance.

Jeremy started to count the seconds between the flash of lightning and the rolling boom of thunder. "One thousand, two thousand, three thousand, four..." he counted in his head, while trying to punch rhythmically to Sensei's count.

"One thousand, two thousand, thr... yup getting closer," thought Jeremy.

Another streaking flash lit up the sky. Jeremy got as far as thinking, "One thou..." before he jumped with fright. The roar of thunder was all around him, shaking the earth, and adding a strangely powerful and charged sense to the air around them.

Sensei let out a loud whoop, his only acknowledgement to the weather, and kept counting.

Lightning struck a lone tree about 50 metres away, and training continued. The thunder was so loud, Jeremy was sure it had split the sky.

Then in the sudden silence, the rain began, almost singing or sighing with a slight hiss as it hit the hot earth. It rained softly at first and then by the bucket load.

Sopping wet, the line of punching students kept on punching.

Even when it started to hail, Sensei kept up a steady count.

Jeremy was standing right behind Sensei and found himself watching the small hailstones bounce off Sensei's head. The ice stones got bigger, and bounced higher. The thunder moved off down the valley, only to be replaced by Jeremy's peals of laughter, as the hail pelted everything brazen enough to be out in the open.

Something about the absurdity or craziness of it all set Jeremy off - laughing shrilly like a hyena at the ice bouncing off Sensei and everything else around him. The laughter broke Sensei's determined focus, and he suddenly declared that it was time for everyone to duck for cover until the storm had passed.

He turns away
To watch in the mirror
Another perspective

WELCOME TO THE POLAR BEAR CLUB

EVERY MORNING RUN ON gasshuku ended with a dip in the nearby dam or river. Sensei always selected his training venues carefully to ensure this was possible. The rule was clothes off and into the water; with the instruction to wait until everyone was at least waist deep. There was a head count, and nobody was allowed out the water until everyone had dunked themselves sufficiently to wet their hair at least once.

For this reason summer gasshukus were always more popular than those held in winter. Although summer meant longer daylight hours and more training in the heat - it also meant no stumbling in the dark on frozen frosty mornings and no freezing in the dam or river water after the morning run.

Gasshuku novices would often mistakenly assume that participation in this sort of thing was optional or voluntary, but Sensei fervently believed that his role as a teacher was not just to teach techniques, but to provide personal challenges for his students to rise above.

In summer, the challenge for many was one of body image. For example, for Vicky, the idea of undressing in front of strangers and streaking into the dam full of self-consciousness was too much to contemplate. She figured that Sensei could not be serious, and slipped off her shoes and socks and entered the water in her running outfit.

The truth was that everyone else was so focused on stripping off as fast as possible and running into the water while not cutting their feet on rocks and stones that they hardly noticed the blur of bodies entering the water. And once submerged in the water there is nothing to see, bar a head bobbing about above the surface.

Vicky almost got away with not stripping down - except for the fact that she walked out of the water in dripping-wet clothing and had no dry clothing to put on after her towel dry. This immediately caught Sensei's attention, and everybody was ordered to strip down and head back into the water. Vicky included. No exceptions.

In winter, Sensei took great delight in the refreshing winter dip and ensured that everyone on gasshuku took part in the polar bear club. Mathew, attending his first gasshuku, had heard about these notorious swims and devised a cunning plan to avoid them.

When everyone gathered at the end of the run and headed off to the dam, Mathew kept his torch off and held back for a minute. Then he quietly slipped off towards the shower block. He figured he'd have a nice warm shower instead of a freezing encounter in the dam - and still have wet hair to make it look as though he had been in the dam.

However, down at the dam, things did not go so well. Everyone else stripped in the dark and entered the inky-black, freezing water with shrieks from the cold, and waited. And waited. Sensei counted 15 heads. Sensei recounted; still only 15 heads.

"Tahmid Sempai and Sergio Sempai, go and check the bungalows. Somebody is missing," said Sensei to two of his senior students. "The rest of you stay in the water, but keep moving to stay warm."

About six minutes later, an embarrassed Mathew emerged flanked by the two Sempai. He was invited to join the rest of the students for a swim. Sensei then said: "Right, everybody out the water, except Mathew. He owes you all another ten minutes."

Mathew stayed in the water, until his teeth were chattering uncontrollably, silently cursing himself for his naivety. He should have realised that decades of teaching training camps meant that Sensei would know every possible cheat and have checks to avoid them.

It didn't take Mathew long to realise that it would have been far less punishing just to man up and get into the cold water the first time.

Sensei took his time getting dressed, keeping a watchful eye on Mathew. When he was finally fully dressed, Sensei said, "Welcome to the polar bear club, Mathew. You can get out now."

Racing thoughts
Suddenly stop
Gasp of cold dam water

A KICK TO THE HEAD

WARREN WAS ONE OF Sensei's more agile students. He moved comfortably and fast, and lived for the many forms of kicks that Sensei taught. Warren put in hours of personal practice honing his skills and perfecting the kicking techniques, to the point that his foot could snap up towards your head in a mawashi geri faster than most of Sensei's students could think of raising an arm or ducking out the way.

Sensei was rather fond of saying: "In combat, you would no more kick to the head that you would punch to the foot." This was usually aimed at lithe Warren, to encourage him to use other techniques despite the fact that the syllabus did, in fact, include a number of kicks that were executed at various target heights, including the head.

This admonition was usually followed by a demonstration by Sensei, where he adeptly intercepted a high kick and held onto the kicking leg, to illustrate how vulnerable someone is when kicking to an upper-level target. Sensei could control the attacker, unbalance the attacker, or sweep them off their feet by attacking the supporting leg, or break the supporting leg's knee. Nasty stuff.

None of this deterred Warren overly much. He found joy in expressing himself through the kicks. While doing randori, he tried to select targets from the waist down and focus on thrusting side kicks to the knee or spinning back kicks to groin or stomach height, but it was inevitable that the odd kick up to the head would slip out, because it was easy, natural, and enjoyable for Warren.

"Warren, would you bend down and punch me on the foot?" asked Sensei, dramatically stopping the class and miming dropping down to punch to the foot, with his head dangerously exposed to a possible attack from knees and hands.

"No, Sensei," said Warren, looking contrite.

"Then why are you wasting precious seconds kicking to the head, rather than punching? Why risk a broken knee, or worse?"

"But, Sensei, why do you teach these techniques if we're not supposed to use them?" asked Warren.

A tense moment passed, but Sensei decided Warren's question was one genuine curiosity rather than insolence.

"I have many functions as a teacher," replied Sensei. "One of them is to train you to develop and use your body to its full potential. Another is to teach you techniques - and yet another is to teach you to use that slow chunk of grey matter between your two ears to judge when it is safe, or wise, to use each of the techniques."

"Most people can't kick very high without a lot of training, so we teach high kicks more to develop the physical skill than with the expectation that these kicks would be used in self-defence - because of the very real dangers I have illustrated over and over again," said Sensei.

"The ability to lift the leg high is needed for more advanced kicks, so see it as more or a progression towards something like this," said Sensei executing an unstoppable dropping axe kick.

His leg moved up above head height in an arc, and powered straight down, with the heel hitting the like an axe blade.

"If you can get your leg up that high, this is generally a safe and effective kick to use. It's not known as the unstoppable thigh of obliteration for nothing," said Sensei.

Warren nodded, part dejected for being the cause of another class lecture, but also suddenly excited to discover yet another kick to learn. "Could you show me that kick again, please Sensei," said Warren, the excitement winning him over.

Releasing
Ego-driven self worth
Practicing kata alone

TRAIN THOSE REFLEXES

MOST OF YOU WOULD be familiar with the saying: Practice makes perfect. Sensei would always encourage his students to practice - but with an emphasis on precision and detail.

"Practice makes permanent, so make sure you practice *correctly*," was one of Sensei's oft-repeated instructions and he often came up with both predictable and inventive new ways to help students ingrain the correct training methods.

One predictable method was Sensei's spinning back kick. It was one of Sensei's signature moves, and it could be relied upon to come out with agonising predictability during randori training, but at a speed just fast enough that all of Sensei's students struggled to avoid it.

Sensei was the third person to pair off with Simon for randori during his brown belt evaluation. Sensei started to turn around for a back kick, and looked over his shoulder at Simon with a glint in his eye. Time went into slow motion for Simon, who knew what was coming, but was unable to avoid the inevitable.

Sensei sent out a back kick, executed with perfect control. Simon was suddenly uprooted from the spot where he seemed to freeze, and he took off and landed in a mangled heap without his undercarriage down.

A year or so later, for Simon's black belt, he had developed his reflexes and sense of self-preservation enough to step back out of range for Sensei's spinning back kick - at least 90 percent of the time.

Apart from landing spinning back kicks with disturbing regularity until Simon figured out an effective counter strategy, Sensei used the opportunity of a dojo move to hone his student's survival skills. Sensei enlisted the help of students to move a load of bricks. He lined the students up on one side of a wall and started randomly throwing bricks over the high wall from the other side for the students to catch.

Simon and his classmates were jumping around trying to stay alive when Sensei's amused face peered over the wall and said: "Good training for reflexes," before resuming the brick throwing exercise.

On another occasion, Sensei wanted to teach Jacques and Mary a sensitivity exercise for t'ai chi. He paired them off, lightly touching hands with just a piece of paper separating their palms. Sensei's instruction was for them to move their hands and arms around while maintaining the lightest of touches to develop a sense of listening and following energy.

In true Sensei style, Jacques and Mary spent many hours working on this drill. Sensei wanted the touch to be so light that the paper fell more often than it stayed between their hands. The paper fell so often during this exercise that Mary, quite unintentionally, developed a chin twitch as a pre-warning to the paper dropping.

The exercise became so ingrained that ten years after stopping this training on a regular basis Mary still feels that tell-tale chin twitch, providing a valuable half-second warning, if she is about to drop her keys, cell phone, or anything; making it much easier to catch or prevent the fall.

Helping the awkward
With patience. Towards progress
Warm appreciative smile

ALWAYS RUN TO THE
TOP OF THE HILL

SENSEI'S STUDENTS OFTEN GO on training runs outside of training time, or occasionally as part of dojo training, in part to improve general fitness and in part develop a strong mind. Sensei claimed that determination is a lot like muscle strength, it needed regular challenges to keep the determination muscles fit, agile, and responsive.

One of Sensei's personal challenges was to always run to the top of Heartbreak Hill. He would never, ever, give up before the summit and walk. Even if he was vomiting as he ran, he would run to the top of the hill.

Sensei also developed strategies to encourage his students to do the same. The first time Jackie encountered the infamous Heartbreak Hill on gasshuku, it didn't take long for her to fall behind, and then slow to a walk.

Sensei knew Jackie was made of sterner stuff and sent two

senior students to run with her and 'encourage' her up the long cement-covered incline. When she slowed to a walk the students, one on each side, dropped a hand to either side of Jackie's buttocks and kept running, forcing her to keep pace and run to the top of the hill, where Sensei was waiting

Sensei was right about Jackie. She was so mortified at being pushed up the hill that the next morning she ran so hard she even passed Sensei on the way up.

Another of Sensei's favourite tricks to encourage students to keep running, or to try harder, was to run in zigzags up the hill in front of them. Mary usually wanted nothing more than to be left to die in peace as she plod-jogged slowly up the hill, but Sensei wouldn't allow that.

There was Sensei, with a bunch of the fitter students, running irritatingly ahead of her, crossing from one side of the road in a zig, back to the other side of the road in a zag. The subtle pressure was awful. Mary constantly felt guilty for being the cause of the longer uphill for everyone else, which made her try harder than she otherwise would choose to.

On other occasions, depending on his reading of the student's ability, Sensei would subtly move the goal posts.

While running up the hill, Sensei would promise students that they could walk as soon as they reached the top - but only if they ran all the way to the top.

But, when they reached the top, they were encouraged to keep on running. "It's downhill now, and you can recover your breath while your legs are moving," Sensei would say, while getting everyone to push past their comfort zone yet again.

Determined running
An uphill slog altered
A burst of orange sunrise

YOU ALWAYS SEE YOUR MISTAKES IN OTHERS

MARY DIDN'T AGREE WITH Sensei all the time. She particularly disagreed with one statement that Sensei used to make, which went along the lines of, "you always see your own mistakes reflected in others". Mary was conscientious and trained hard. She was quite confident that she could spot mistakes that she was not guilty of, thank you very much.

The statement was, of course, a generalisation, meaning that people more readily see the mistakes others make than they are able to see the same mistakes or flaws in themselves. Mary could accept that paraphrased statement, but it still irked her when Sensei would insist that students could *only* see their own mistakes in others.

But one day she got to witness Sensei's statement in action.

Mary had only had limited exposure to push hands training. Sensei's t'ai chi focus was on health and meditation, and Mary only discovered push hands when she had travelled to train with other instructors as Sensei suggested. So when one of Sensei's former students, who was now seriously studying t'ai chi overseas, came to visit, Sensei suggested that Mary might like to do some additional informal training.

Geoff was fit and strong, and a keen surfer and skier, in addition to his t'ai chi training, and Mary met up with him at the dojo; looking forward to a friendly exchange of skills.

Geoff obviously trained at a dojo that had quite a competitive streak, thought Mary observing that he was more intent on winning and uprooting Mary than he was on training and learning.

Despite his natural strength advantage and extensive push hands training, Geoff was using his strength, rather than t'ai chi principles, to push Mary around.

Mary tried all the skills she knew. She softened her arms to make it hard for Geoff to pull or push her. She bent her knees and tried to root when he pulled. Instead of the light touch that Mary was used to - to allow people of all levels to learn and grow without being dominated - Geoff used his physical strength, as opposed to internal alignment, softness, and actual t'ai chi skill.

While under no illusion as to her lack of skills in push hands, Mary knew that Geoff was not approaching training as he should. In frustration, Mary resorted to using physical strength herself, just to show Geoff what it was like to be on the receiving end of the t'ai chi equivalent of bullying.

The first time she applied strength and resisted Geoff's push and pushed him off balance in return, Geoff responded with, "That's not t'ai chi."

"Welcome to my world," thought Mary, followed by "Oh,

that's *exactly* what Sensei, meant," as she looked at her watch and made a lame excuse of running out of time to escape any further interactions with Geoff.

It wasn't the first time that Mary observed that you learn something from every person you get to interact with. Sometimes you learn what to do, and at times like this, you learn what not to do. Both are valuable lessons, even if it does not always feel like it at the time.

Cotton-wrapped steel
Yields and melds into fa jing
Hot summer's evening

MONKEY PICKS A PEACH

SENSEI'S IMPROMPTU TALKS IN class were usually riveting, either because the topic and Sensei's knowledge was fascinating or because Sensei was in warrior lecture mode and nobody dared breathe or move.

One lesson that John remembers in vivid detail is Sensei's 'monkey picks a peach' talk. Sensei used this to describe a type of grab where the opponent is so focused on the grab, like a monkey picking a peach, that you can use this intent against them.

Sensei painted the scene. It involved a monkey, a large glass jar with a narrow neck, and a tempting piece of fruit in the jar. The neck of that jar was large enough for the fruit to pass through, but not large enough to allow someone, or some monkey, to pull the fruit out while holding it.

As you would expect, said Sensei, "The monkey will want to get at the fruit, and he'll stick his hand through the neck of the jar. He will reach down and grab the nearest peach with a string of saliva dribbling down his chin, like the drool on your granny's chin when you have to give her a peck hello."

"The monkey will try, in vain, to get the peach out of the jar. Pulling and pulling, but he won't let go of that peach. The monkey is effectively trapped by his desire for the peach. Some will eventually let go, but some monkeys will die of starvation, or get caught by hunters using this method as a trap; despite it being within the monkey's power to drop the fruit and escape.

"People can get trapped by their desires in much the same way," said Sensei.

Some attackers will move to grab you. When they succeed, they will be intent on holding onto you. You can use this focus against them like this," instructed Sensei, indicating to John to grab his extended wrist.

"Now, John here, has grabbed me and he wants to use this grab to stay in control. If he's got my arm in his hand, he only has one other arm to worry about. Now, I'm going to threaten John's grip a little, like this," continued Sensei, while turning his palm to face upward.

"You can see this new position has weakened John's grip and created an opening I can pull out of, between the thumb and fingers. This will make John hold on tighter, like a monkey with that peach. As he grips even tighter, I can start to pull John off balance by pulling him towards me. Then, by suddenly changing direction and using a thumb break, like this," said Sensei, showing how he could trap John's thumb between his palms by sliding his left hand under the right up to the point of the grab.

"Then, it's easy to throw John off and get the hell out of harm's way. Most untrained attackers, if they are able to grab onto you, they will try to *keep* a hold of you. This has many advantages in combat. It's worth remembering that your peach could be any desire or belief - this is not limited to combat. In many ways, we're no more evolved than monkeys," said Sensei.

A teacher's function:
Hold the mirror up for you
Autumn reflections

THERE IS ONLY THE RIGHT WAY

SENSEI DID HAVE A few crazy years in his wild and carefree youth where he smoked, but if you ask him today, he would tell you he never smoked. It was a time long before he tried to turn his passion for scuba diving into a living, only to find it ruined the joy found in the freedom of diving.

It's not that Sensei is deliberately telling a lie. His brief affair with that cancer-causing addiction did not last long, and Sensei quickly realised that he had made a bad decision and moved on. It's the way Sensei worked.

He did not believe in dwelling on past mistakes. He simply decided to improve and adopted the better option. This extended to training too. If Sensei's training and research uncovered a new and better way of doing things, Sensei's training changed, without warning.

It was a habit that annoyed Mary beyond words when it

happened to affect her training.

Sensei was pedantic; students were left in no doubt what so ever as to what was expected of them in training. So when Sensei discovered a better way of doing something and changed a technique, diligent students like Mary were caught in a difficult dilemma.

Respect and courtesy would mean that it would be inappropriate to question Sensei on the dojo floor, but the technique was so obviously different that it warranted an explanation. Mary would try a subtle: "Sensei, I thought we were supposed to do the move like this..." while showing the old way.

"Nonsense," Sensei would reply. "We've always done it this way," while showing the new move. A few of the senior students would smile knowingly, which annoyed Mary even more.

Mary knew better than to argue the point. The rationale for the new way of moving would usually come out in class within a couple of weeks, but it still frustrated Mary that Sensei would not admit it was a new change.

After Sensei returned from a three-month training session in Japan, he introduced a bunch of changes. The first was a shorter stance. Up until Sensei's departure the students were encouraged to be as athletic as possible to improve their agility and leg strength. No stance could ever be too long as it helped you move dynamically into and out of sword range.

On Sensei's return, the stances were shortened. Considerably.

Sensei imported about four hideous, black, weighted vests and had people train with them on. They weighed 20kgs when filled with the unpleasant smelling clay weights. Then the rationale was slowly revealed.

"If you're wearing 20kgs or more of armour, like the samurai would have done on the battlefield, all day, you're going to need to conserve energy. If you're out in the wild, not on the smooth dojo floor, do you really think you'll be able to slide out of range like a graceful ballerina?" said Sensei.

This particular set of kata was designed for battlefield use, against people wearing armour - so we train as though we are wearing armour explained Sensei.

Every now and then, Mary's well-ingrained long stance would come out in training, and Sensei would snap something like: "Shorten that stance, Mary. There is only the right way to train."

Mary would fume quietly to herself, but over the years she came to understand that this was Sensei's way of denying the power of past ingrained habits. He would pretend they did not exist and try to train as though he had always done the new correct version. From that point she was able to join the seniors with their knowing smile when the next change came along.

Tragic conditions
Gnawing at inner peace
Go walk the dog

THE POWER OF SOFTNESS

THE POWER OF SOFTNESS is one of those martial arts concepts that appear to be counterintuitive. How can being soft equate to being strong and powerful? It is the sort of statement that doesn't make sense until you experience it.

Whether it was push hands, sensitivity exercises, or randori Sensei would insist that everyone try to work as slowly and softly as possible. "You can never be too soft," Sensei would say. It wasn't true for everyone, but that generalisation was correct for the majority of students. The hardest part was to learn to respond softly, then it was easy to respond with hardness, the proverbial steel bar wrapped in cotton wool, when the occasion warranted it.

The theory went something like this. If your techniques relied on strength alone, the strongest person would always win - and there will always be someone out there who was bigger and stronger than you. It is the power of softness that allowed you to find the edge that David found over Goliath.

Sensei would also illustrate the problems with a tense and rigid arm, coming in for a punch, as an example. An arm with tense muscles would be slow to respond and recover if the opponent deflected the arm. Deflecting the fist itself would work to send it off target, but Sensei would show that it only takes a gentle push on the elbow or shoulder for the punch to miss the target by a healthy margin.

"When you use strength, it is difficult for you to change direction or target if you miss. Much like a bullet hurtling out of a gun, it either hits the target or misses and expends its energy regardless," said Sensei.

"A rigid arm also provides a skilled opponent with lots of leverage," Sensei said. "Nick, punch towards my chest."

As Nick punched, Sensei deftly stepped back as he deflected a punch, grabbed Nick's wrist and brought his other hand up under the elbow as he stepped in closer. With a subtle roll of the arm at the elbow Sensei applied an elbow bar that had Nick on his knees and tapping out.

"Now if Nick applied the power of softness at just the right moment, I wouldn't be able to apply that elbow bar," said

Sensei signalling Nick to punch again.

In slow motion, Sensei stepped back, deflected the punch and went to grab the wrist.

"Now soften your arm a little. Good. You can already see that it is harder for me to control Nick's arm. When Nick sees my hand coming up to his elbow, he knows to anticipate an elbow bar by using softness. If he appears to go with me as I push the elbow over, but then accelerates just a little ahead, he can roll out of the elbow bar before I have had a chance to apply it," said Sensei as Nick followed Sensei's instructions.

"Pair off quickly," announced Sensei as everyone rushed to form two lines. "The side facing the shomen, step forward with the right leg and punch towards the chest with a rigid right arm. Now, the other side step back with left leg on a 45 degree angle, intercept the punch with the right arm and grab the wrist. Step the left leg forward and apply an elbow bar. No, like this..."

"Good. Now the other side punching," continued Sensei as the class swapped roles several times until everyone had the hang of how to apply the elbow bar.

"Now I want you to soften your punching arm and roll out of that arm bar. Ichi," began Sensei, counting for the punching side to start their punch. "As you feel that hand on your elbow, go with it and then speed up. Good."

When both sides had evaded the elbow bar a few times, Sensei said: "Here is another example. If my torso is rigid and Nick pushes on my shoulder, I can try and resist it. But the harder Nick pushes, the harder it is for me to resist."

"Now give a *really* hard push," Sensei said to Nick.

Nick gave a hard push on one shoulder, which moved Sensei backwards a step or two, leaving him fighting for balance.

"Now if my torso is relaxed and soft, I can yield with that push," pointed out Sensei as Nick came in with another push. "And, if I'm smart, I can use all of Nick's hard power to my advantage." He rotated his body with the push, allowing the shoulder Nick pushed to move back and turn his body. Sensei simultaneously stuck out a leg, tripping Nick up as his forward trajectory carried him past Sensei.

"That's the power of softness," said Sensei.

Sunrise through the window
Distracts from the kneeling bow
Smiling I return to now

DOJO CUISINE

SENSEI ALWAYS MAINTAINED THAT the body was a complex chemical factory and deserved to be fed the best and most appropriate food, to gain the best results. At the time, Sensei's stated goal was to live his 125th birthday, and he used many opportunities around dojo festivities and training events to inculcate better nutritional and eating habits amongst his students.

Fizzy cold drinks were banned, long before bottled water was sold in stores, let alone became a fashion item. Cigarettes and drugs were likely to earn you expulsion. Chips and crisps were labelled junk food, and sugar was high on the 'should be avoided' list, long before sugar free diets came out. Alcohol was also on the banned list - because of its ability to negatively affect the brain (seriously - read the scientific research).

New students planning for a 'bring and share' event at the

dojo were often confounded by the long list of things not to bring. Salads replaced a packet of crisps, fruit was offered instead of those tempting cream doughnuts. Only 100% natural, unsweetened fruit juice would pass the Sensei test - and that was diluted 50:50 with water to prevent a fructose rush.

Saturday morning training often ended with a welcome class smoothie, with everyone contributing some fresh fruit or yoghurt for some of the best tasting smoothies ever consumed (somehow things always taste better after a hard workout).

At one stage, Sensei also introduced a bring-and-share breakfast on a Saturday morning after class - again hoping to encourage people to eat wisely and healthily for the most important meal of the day. This generally went well, but there was always someone who didn't quite get the message and brought in a tempting tray of chocolate muffins.

But Mario, a t'ai chi student, in his 60s at the time, presented Sensei with the most confounding breakfast. He brought something healthy - an interesting fruit salad - but soaked the fruit in rum before making the fruit salad, as he always did, to improve the flavour. Sensei had taken a few mouthfuls before he realised and spat the remainder out. Mario blamed his Italian roots.

A spring fast was almost always an annual event on the dojo calendar. Sensei would encourage everyone to sign up and take part. The idea was to detox the body and provide it with a clean start. Participants would pick one day a week, for four weeks, as their fast day on which they would only consume water. The following day, the fast was broken with fruit juice, or later with a coarsely chewed banana and lemon juice. Followed by fruit over the course of the morning, a light salad for lunch, some nuts as a mid-afternoon snap and a healthy vegetable soup for the evening meal (no bread).

Everyone was encouraged to eat healthy foods for the rest of the week and the cycle would begin again for the second, third, and fourth week. Usually the whole process of detoxing from sugar, caffeine, and other substances was enough to encourage students to make healthier eating choices for longer periods.

Gasshuku was another time that students discovered the delights of dojo cuisine. Nobody was allowed to bring any food or drinks with them to gasshuku. Even vitamin tablets and medication had to be handed in to Sensei to avoid any false claims that someone seen swallowing something was just taking a tablet.

Gasshuku food was healthy, and often a culture shock for new comers, especially for those with limited experience in the kitchen - as everyone took turns to prepare meals in teams.

After the daily run and swim, the kitchen duty team would prepare a fresh fruit salad, with a minimum of five different fruits, which they dutifully served to everyone else while they did their morning stretch session on mats on the lawn.

Then it was breakfast in the dining room, with copious amounts of rooibos or ginger tea. Breakfast was initially a healthy mix of muesli and yoghurt, or toast and sugar-free jam, honey, cheese, and other approved spreads eaten to the sounds of general chatter, or Sensei reading a chapter from a book he had decided to share for that gasshuku. Scrambled eggs were always popular when they were on the menu.

Gasshuku meals were almost always entirely vegetarian, but after about 2010, Sensei changed breakfasts to a rice and fish meal, prompted by his experiences of meals when training in Japan, and on nutritional research about what an optimal meal to break the evening fast was.

Next up was a refreshment break at around 10am - usually diluted fruit juice. Then lunch at around 12:30 - with healthy salads in various forms, and the occasional indulgence with pizza slices or an open toasted cheese if it was a particularly hard training day.

The mid-afternoon refreshment break was the last task for the out-going kitchen duty team, and a new team would take over to prepare the evening meal. The first evening meal on gasshuku was always a vegetable soup. Spaghetti was another staple because, at least in theory, everyone knows how to cook spaghetti.

One on particular gasshuku Andrew Sempai's team managed to produce a hard glutinous slush out of several boxes of spaghetti - apparently it *did* stick to the kitchen ceiling after being heated in a dry pan with oil and then boiled to twenty minutes. This meal reportedly tested Sensei's resolve that everybody ate what was served up on their plate, but that rule was still deemed immutable. The tasteless spaghetti, with a texture of hard rubber, was cut up small and swallowed down with lots of tea.

On rare occasions, there would be Milo in the evenings, or the odd treat such as a birthday cake if someone was celebrating a birthday, or ice cream, usually around the third of fourth day when everyone's motivation slumped.

With little exposure to their usual consumption of meat, sweets, cold sodas, cigarettes, and alcohol there were usually two camps of people at the end of gasshuku. Those who were planning their first stop at the nearest fast food outlet on the drive home and discussing how far from the gasshuku venue they would need to be before it was safe to light up, and those who were motivated to keep the healthy habit going a little bit longer.

For most participants, many of Sensei suggested healthier ways became more of a way of life - at least after they had attended their second or third gasshuku. It was, literally, food for thought.

The swoosh of a blade
Cutting through air then
Bird song clear as a temple bell

RED SASH

JUST UNDER TWO YEARS after Jacques and Mary were awarded their black sash, they found they had been nominated for their red sash evaluation. Sensei had given them little instruction other than saying, "You need to know the sequence and the breathing very well - on both left and right sides. And you need to know, and be able to demonstrate, the applications for the moves."

The evaluation was set for a Saturday afternoon in December. When pressed, Sensei told them to allow a couple of hours for the evaluation.

Saturday finally dawned, and the slightly nervous pair arrived early as expected. They handed in their membership books and started warming up at the back of the dojo. It wasn't long before the evaluation started, with Sensei sitting eagle-eyed behind his table surrounded by sheets and sheets of paper spread out in front of him.

"Mary," he said. "Show me the fifth single whip."

"Left or right hand side, Sensei - and does that include or exclude the diagonal, horizontal, and extended single whips?" asked Mary, as she visualised and ran through the laminated training prompts she had stuck to her shower walls. "Oh, and do you want it with breathing, Sensei?"

Sensei raised one eyebrow ever so slightly, a little surprised by the confident response. He had expected that students would have to mentally run through the form to find the correct move. "How may single whips are there?" asked Sensei.

Sensei could see that Mary was about to answer without hesitation, so he changed tack. "Jacques?" he said, leaving Mary with her mouth opening and closing soundlessly, like a goldfish, as she squashed the ready answer that was about to come out.

"There are nine, excluding diagonal and horizontal single whip - and two of the nine are extended single whips," answered Jacques.

Sensei's one eyebrow lifted a little higher. "How many are in each section and what moves do they follow?" he asked, shifting his gaze to Mary.

"One in section one, two in section two and six in section three - excluding the horizontal and diagonal whips - which are one each in sections two and three. They all start after grasp sparrow's tail, except for three that follow wave hands like clouds," said Mary.

About a year ago, Sensei had suggested that his students draw up a spreadsheet and analyse all the moves in the form. He didn't really expect that anyone would bother, but clearly Jacques and Mary had risen to the challenge - and it was paying off.

"Mary, show me the fifth including all the whips on the left. Jacques, give me the fifth excluding diagonal and horizontal on the right hand side - with breathing, both of you," said Sensei, who went on to pick move after move from the Yang long form for about an hour.

"Mary, take a seat. Jacques, I want you to just breathe naturally and tell me when you start to breathe in and out." Sensei pulled out a metronome and set it to Jacques' breathing rhythm.

"Good. Now give me the t'ai chi form on the right hand side, but you have to time it so that each move is completed to the metronome-set breathing cycle. Do you understand?"

Jacques blinked hard, taking in the implications of this new curve ball. Usually the breathing slowed or sped up based on the move being done. With the requirement reversed, Jacques would need to speed up or slow down the moves to meet a standardised timing.

"Begin," said Sensei, and Jacques started the form, mind racing ahead to figure out where he needed to speed up and slow down. It was a difficult 40 minutes of concentration and Jacques was soaked in sweat, but felt he had managed well enough.

"Mary. Your turn," said Sensei. Once he'd set the dreaded the metronome to Mary's breathing cycle he said: "Since you've had the advantage of watching Jacques, give me the form on the left hand side."

Mary gulped and prepared to start.

"Begin," said Sensei. She started well, but struggled to do the mirror image of the form and adjust to moving slower or faster as dictated by the breathing for each part of the technique. After a few moves where she had to rush very un-t'ai chi like at the end of a move to fit it, in Mary found a solution. She started to count to four in her head, breaking the metronome count down - and adjusting the move so that she was a quarter done, half done, almost finished and finished.

After that 'Aha! Moment', her form flowed more like t'ai chi should, and probably made the difference between a pass and a floundering fail.

Now almost hours into the evaluation, Sensei moved onto the applications. Again he randomly selected a move, and asked for an explanation of the application, and then a demonstration of the application, alternating in a randomised fashion between the pair on the floor. Occasionally, he would ask for a second or third possible application for a move.

Giving an explanation of the application was relatively easy. Demonstrating it required a deeper level of knowledge, which wasn't always obvious when watching Sensei in class. He would tell his partner how to grab or attack, so that the particular application would work - and that knowledge was what Jacques and Mary needed to demonstrate too.

Four-and-a-half hours after the start of the evaluation, the pair were mentally and emotionally exhausted when Sensei said, "Right. Take a seat at a desk." There were two desks set up at opposite ends of the dojo, with an exam pad, a pen, and a sheet with questions on each.

Jacques and Mary shared a glance, both registering surprise. They glanced at the clock, and tried to focus while anticipating the response from their respective irate partners waiting at home. They weren't expecting the theory component as well, although perhaps they ought to have known to expect the unexpected with Sensei.

Dragonfly darting
Silver snatches of sunlight
Escape the sword blade

AFTERWORD

SENSEI SUFFERED A massive stroke on 9 September 2015, damaging the back right quarter of his brain and affecting the functioning of the left side of his body. This has limited, but not entirely eliminated, Sensei's life-lessons which continue to entertain a small handful of students who train with Sensei at home.

Sensei is re-learning how to walk, and hopes - at some stage - to be able to regain some functioning in his left had. Recovery from a stroke is slow - painfully slow - and has been a steep learning curve for someone who believed that mind over matter could fix anything.

If you have trained with Sensei and have a story you would like to share we'd love to include it in a second volume of <u>Lessons from the dojo</u>. Just drop Shaz a line and let her know.

If you've enjoyed these lessons and would like to support Bob in his recovery, there is an option on YouCaring - contact Shaz for the link.

Thank you for sharing some training memories and life lessons with us. We hope you enjoyed the read and we would appreciate a review on Amazon if you have a minute or two to spare.

I can't keep going
But I don't know how to stop
A tender caress

ABOUT SENSEI

BOB Davies, or Sensei in this book, was born in Pretoria, South Africa, but spent most of his time in Cape Town and Durban, before moving to New Zealand in 2010. He began training in various styles of traditional and sport karate in 1967, was awarded his South African Springbok colours in 1984, and achieved the ranking level of 5th Dan by 1985. During this period he also studied aikido, jujutsu and kobudo (traditional Okinawan weapons).

In 1985 Bob decided that the worldwide trend of commercialisation and modification of training for sport and competition was not conducive to effective self-defence application, health and personal growth, and withdrew his support for the modern sport-variants of the arts.

Since then he immersed himself in the Chinese civilian defensive art systems, with particular emphasis on wing chun kung fu, tang shou dao, t'ai chi ch'uan, chin na, and hsing i-ch'uan. At the same time, Bob also studied the Philippine fighting systems of escrima, kali and arnis de mano.

From 1995 onwards, Bob undertook advanced training in the classical Japanese martial weapons' arts of jo, sword, spear, long staff, and naginata as well as the original Chinese/Okinawan civilian unarmed combative defence arts of todejutsu and koryu uchinadi.

Bob is a long-standing member of a number of dedicated research groups including the International Ryukyu Karate Research Society, and the International Hoplology Society.

Bob opened his first teaching and training centre in Durban, South Africa, in January 1975 followed by a full-time dojo in 1977, and developed a provincial organisation of eleven branches over the next decade. His studies have taken him to Japan, Hong Kong, Taiwan, Singapore, Philippines, Australia, Western and Eastern Europe and the USA. Balancing this expertise has included an in-depth examination of some of the 'healing' aspects of martial and civilian combat arts training provided by a number of schools of meditation, Shiatsu, Chinese Chi-Kung, as well as clinical anatomy and physiology including a year of full-time cadaver dissection.

Known as Lao Tze (Chinese for teacher) to his students, Bob has personally trained more than 6000 students and developed more than sixty-five black belts (in four different disciplines) of whom twelve have reached the internationally rated rank of 3rd Dan, four the rank of 4th Dan, and one the rank of 5th Dan.

His practical expertise resulted in Bob holding the position of specialist instructor for the Durban City Police from 1986 for a period of 13 years; responsible for training force members in all aspects of the use of batons, self-defence techniques, arrest restraints, close-quarter combat, compliance, restraint and come-along techniques. Between

1987 and 1989 instruction also involved special Riot and Crowd control training as well as the use of the standard issue PR24 baton. In 1995, Bob also ran an advanced training course for a selected group of senior instructors of the South African Police Services and members of their Special Task Force, incorporating a number of practical scenarios.

Realising the importance of maintaining a functional balance between his physical conflict management skills and the needs of local and international business communities encouraged Bob to pursue his studies in various management programmes over the years, acquiring his first business degree in 1974; Bob has since completed his M+5 in Business Practice and his Honours degree in Psychology at the University of Canterbury in New Zealand in 2014

Always one to lead from the front, Bob unexpectedly suffered a massive stroke in September 2015. This has curtailed a lot of his teaching but he still holds small classes in Oxford for a handful of dedicated students.

If you would like to get in touch, you can contact Bob on:
bob@wu-shin.com
www.wu-shin.com

ABOUT THE AUTHOR

SHAZ Davis was born in Durban, South Africa, but after more than four decades she decided that the colder climes of New Zealand held more appeal, and moved at the end of 2009. She now lives in the small community of Oxford, on the country's South Island, with her partner, Bob (Sensei in this book), and their dog, Shanti.

After completing a commerce degree at the University of KwaZulu-Natal she continued with law but dropped out in her second year, when she realised that justice wasn't the black and white truth she believed it would be.

Shaz started her writing career focusing on the security and travel incentives industry. She then spent time as a reporter on a community newspaper, before becoming editor and publication manager for the South Africa Sugar Association. After that she spent more than a decade as a freelance journalist.

She has written many articles for magazines and online publication, both in SA and NZ, as well as for the UK-based SciDev.net for science articles - two of which won awards in the online category in 2008 and 2009. She was also part of a small team to win the NetGuide Award for the best website for small business in New Zealand from 2010 to 2012.

Two of her three books on t'ai chi are available on Kindle and she is planning to release them on Create Space very shortly as well.

Shaz currently works from home for a network of independently-owned hostels throughout NZ, but when she has time to herself she enjoys being out in the mountains, improving her photography skills, and making homemade natural soaps.

She began training with Sensei in 1997 and holds a black belt in the Japanese sword art of katori shinto ryu and a read sash in t'ai chi, which she teaches locally in Oxford.

Shaz spends much of her time caring for Bob, or playing frisbee with Shanti, but one thing is certain - she will continue to write for a long time to come.

You can reach Shaz on:

sharon@sharondavis.co
www.sharondavis.co
Twitter: @shazster